Chasing Sanity

PINKY HARTNETT

Chasing Sanity
A Memoir about living with Bipolar Disorder

INSPIRED
PUBLISHING

Chasing Sanity
A Memoir about living with Bipolar Disorder
First Edition, First Impression 2022
ISBN: 978-0-6397-2950-3
Copyright © Pinky Hartnett

Published by: Inspired Publishing
PO Box 82058 | Southdale | 2135 Johannesburg, South Africa
Email: info@inspiredpublishing.co.za
www.inspiredpublishing.co.za

Table of Contents

Dedication

This book is dedicated to all the women and young girls, who may be struggling to get out of bed in the morning, anxious about facing the world. We are surrounded by many who can no longer cope with life due to mental illness. This book is a reminder that they are not alone, there's always someone who is willing to listen and help. Whether you are struggling with depression, bipolar disorder, anxiety, schizophrenia or suicidal thoughts; the bottom line is that we all deserve to be treated with dignity, care, patience and understanding. We walk this journey together!

When I was writing this book, it felt like I have finally found my voice, after years of struggling in silence and I hope that those who are struggling can also find their own voice. It is also my hope that all those who are suffering due to mental illness, may find the path towards their healing. In a strange way, my source of healing has come from sharing my story in this book.

Diagnosing mental illness is often difficult, but once you find a good psychiatrist and psychologist, one has a better chance of coping with mental health. Once you are prescribed medication, it is very important to take your medication because that's one of the many ways you can bring a balance into your life. It's important to look out for outlets that can help you simplify your life and do things in small doses rather than taking on more than you can manage. Even though one can be afflicted with mental illness, life can still become manageable and you can enjoy a fruitful life with a purpose. Let's come together and educate one another about mental wellness and share experiences that will allow us to learn from each other. Finally, I hope that this book will raise awareness about mental health as well as encourage people to share their own stories.

Acknowledgements

I would like to thank my husband Fintan for his patience, love and support through out this journey. It wouldn't have been possible to go through my journey of healing without him holding my hand. I am always humbled whenever you remind me that we are a team and that life is "not a sprint but a marathon." To my children, Hope, Aidan and Connor, thank you for being my biggest cheerleaders, for teaching me about life and inspiring me to be the best version of myself.

To my mother Nomathemba Mazaleni, thank you for believing in me and for inspiring me at every turn. I'm grateful to my mom for constantly reassuring me that I can do it. When I felt overwhelmed with the writing, my mom reminded me to take it easy and asked me to remember why I'm on this journey to begin with. Thank you so much Mama, for asking me difficult yet necessary questions.

I would also like to thank my cousin Siyasanga Mabukane for all the support he has given me. I'm so grateful to him for allowing me to bounce off book ideas with him and especially for being a good listener. Thank you, Siyasanga for reminding me that I'm more than capable of sharing my story in a way that impacts others.

I would like to acknowledge my sister-in-law Kate Hartnett for checking in every week to see how the book is coming along. Thank you for the candid conversations that always remind me that I'm appreciated and I matter. I can't thank you enough for welcoming us into your home and for being a second mom to my boys, you are truly amazing!

Lastly, I would like to thank my friend, Namhla Zama Qata for being my conscience and critic. We've come a long way since our East London days. I'm so grateful to you for always giving me constructive criticism and for encouraging me to reach for the stars. Women like you are truly a beacon of hope and it's in the way you effortlessly give yourself to others that makes you a remarkable woman.

Prologue

For the longest time - before being diagnosed with bipolar mood disorder I struggled to understand what was wrong with me. It was a question which kept me on an emotional rollercoaster for years. At that time, I honestly thought what was happening to me, was unique to only me. Whenever I tried to make sense of my situation, particularly those related to my mood swings and general behavior, I would become despondent and feel depressed. I had no diagnosis then, but I knew something was not quite right.

I realize now that this process is not unique to me or my temperament, but that it happens to so many who struggle with mental disorders.

According to Our World in Data, in 2017, the number of people living with bipolar disorder were estimated at 46 million worldwide. Out of that number, about 20% of South Africans will experience a depressive disorder. This number is very likely much higher when we take into consideration the countries where diagnosis is difficult because of poverty and the limited access to mental health resources. I say this, not to glorify the numbers, but only to remind you that you are not alone.

In the 1990's there were few well documented cases of people living with bipolar disorder in South Africa, though a reasonable estimate is that somewhere between 3% - 5% of South Africans were and are afflicted with this mood disorder. As a result, so many of us just fell through the cracks and suffered in silence. Which is probably why bipolar disorder can be so destructive, and why: *"bipolar disorder results in 9.2 years reduction in expected life span, and as many as one in five patients with bipolar disorder commit suicide."* (National Institute of Mental Health).

While diagnosing mental disorders has never been an exact science it is also difficult to accept the diagnosis if it applies to you, and even harder to start, and continue with treatment. However, taking the right medication and exploring various therapies can change the quality of life for the better, ensuring that people suffering from bipolar disorder are able to live a full and balanced life.

I was in my early thirties, when I was conclusively diagnosed with bipolar disorder. Although the warning signs were there for a long time, the diagnosis shook me to my core. It never occurred to me that I would be someone living with bipolar disorder, or manic depression, as it is also known. I'm not sure if I even understood what it was at the time. I did not know what the implications were or how the diagnosis would translate into my everyday life and most importantly how I would have to adjust my life to live with it. In a space of 6 years my life changed drastically, I went from being manic to being depressed. Manic episodes may include symptoms such as high energy, reduced need for sleep and loss of touch with reality. Depressive episodes may include symptoms such as low energy, low motivation and loss of interest in daily activities. Mood episodes last days to months at a time and may also be associated with suicidal thoughts.

I went from taking bipolar medication to finally adjusting to a routine which fit my lifestyle. Over the years I learned to be *deliberate* when it comes to dealing with my illness. Now, I am committed to taking my medication, as well as using holistic therapies, such as having an exercise routine, eating healthy, and educating myself about mental health. One of the things that keeps me in check, is regularly getting psychotherapy which always helps me. I love it, because it helps me track my progress in the battle with this disorder.

I have often come across people who have had to deal with one form of mental illness or another, and I always thought those people are so brave. At times I've also seen people poke fun at those who suffer from mental illness. Such people are unkind, mean, ignorant and downright insensitive. We should always remember that having a mental disorder is not your fault nor is it a punishment handed down from above. It is genetics and chemistry run amok, out of your immediate control. At times both these external and internal factors will have an impact on the person struggling with mental illness and make their life and the lives of those around them very difficult indeed.

When I first drafted this book, I thought deeply and extensively about the stigma which is often associated with mental illness and how, it has unfortunately subjected so many people to so much discrimination over the years. I now realize that this stigma is far-reaching, nuanced and very cruel, especially since people who suffer from mental illness have no control over their disorder - that is, until they take medication prescribed by a psychiatrist or a doctor.

I feel it is important for me to write this book, because I hope to inspire other people—especially young African women. Because of the staunch patriarchy found in traditional African families, the socio-economic status and society in general, African woman have a more difficult task, in firstly, recognizing mental illness, and secondly having the freedom to seek the appropriate medical attention. I have found that African women in particular are, more often than not, silenced, rather than encouraged to speak about mental illness.

I hope that this book will be used as a stepping stone for the understanding and acceptance of one's own mental health status. Many people struggle to come to terms with their diagnosis and mental illness.

I want this book to be evidence that you can be afflicted with this disorder and still live a 'normal', fruitful, and healthy life.

Life is complex enough and it is even more challenging when you are forced to navigate the intricate winding road, that is unstable mental health. Even though I am dealing with this – and it does become quite hectic sometimes – does not mean I cannot enjoy my life. The critical thing for me is to find the balance that works for me, which means I consciously take into account my treatment and my everyday living. I recognize that while bipolar disorder can be challenging the possibilities to be my best self are endless. They can be for you as well.

This book is for both the sufferers and non-sufferers alike, to help them take control of their lives, encourage them to get a medical assessment if necessary and to help those in roles of support, assist them as they strive for good mental health. Bipolar disorder can easily take you on a downward spiral, but it is through your understanding of mental health that you can generate a shift in your thoughts, actions and most importantly in how you create dialogues with other people and raise awareness about mental health.

My ambition with this book is to help people identify the early warning signs of bipolar disorder and seek medical intervention as soon as possible. There are various organizations that work tirelessly to support people living with mental illness, use them. There is indeed a distortion between the reality of the illness and what people think they know about someone afflicted with a mood disorder. It is without a doubt, very difficult to accurately diagnose bipolar disorder, let alone prescribe the proper medication. But without a diagnosis, it cannot be treated effectively. I do believe that governments around the world could work harder on addressing this issue. However, we all have a responsibility to equip ourselves with knowledge and understanding about mental health if we want to navigate this crazy world, we live in.

Most importantly, what I wanted to achieve with this book, is to let the experiences I highlight raise awareness about the impact bipolar disorder has on individuals and the people they love. Mine is an African voice because, contrary to traditional belief, bipolar disorder affects Africans as well.

CHAPTER 1

To Insanity and Beyond

"Don't worry if people think you're crazy. You are crazy. You have that kind of intoxicating insanity that lets other people dream outside of the lines and become who they're destined to be." ~**Jennifer Elisabeth**

I grew up in the 1980s, shuttling between the second biggest township in South Africa, Mdantsane, and tiny Gwali, which is a rural Xhosa speaking village outside Alice in the Eastern Cape formerly known as the Ciskei. Mdantsane back then was nothing short of a ticking time bomb, fueled by the intense political turmoil in the country. Hope and optimism for a better tomorrow lingered in the polluted air, but the same air reeked of so much fear and uncertainty, rendering our futures as dusty and bleak as the township we lived in. This was the harsh reality of life for a Black child in Apartheid South Africa. Moving between my parent's house in Mdantsane and my grandparents' house in Gwali was a mission. It was common to drive through rolling roadblocks which worked as identification document control stations designed to ferret out any underground political activity. Before we reached a checkpoint, my grandmother would urge my cousin Siyasanga and I to be quiet and behave ourselves so that we didn't get into trouble with the police. It seemed like forever travelling to Gwali. We could sense the fear in my grandparents at the sight of the heavily armed white men on the roads, as we made our way north.

Due to the wave of township school uprisings – which had been ongoing throughout the country since the mid-1970s - my parents made the final decision that Siyasanga and I would go and live with my grandparents, in Gwali, for a period of 2 years. I was in tears upon hearing this, but I tried to understand things from their point of view. It was a dark and turbulent time for me as a child, and the logic behind living in the rural village, was to shield me from the unpredictable bouts of insurgency - and the possibility of a violent death. My parents stood no chance of outsmarting the system, especially with poverty intensifying its hold over us, choking any real efforts my parents made toward clawing their way out of the bottomless pit that was the township.

Gwali is one of many villages on the outskirts of the town of Alice and this is where I received my primary schooling. Road R345 is a tarred road, and it is the only road that takes you anywhere near Gwali. If you follow this road, it will take you up the mountain to the picturesque Hogsback. Popular for having the most incredible waterfalls, as well as its snow in winter, it is frequented by tourists from all over South Africa. The villages along the road are amazing to see because of the multitude of brightly painted houses. But instead of driving all the way to Hogsback that day, we took a sharp left turn by the orange farm. My cousin Siyasanga and I marveled at those oranges, at how big, juicy and bright they looked. It was such a delightfully mesmerizing sight which drew you in. The journey to Gwali from the highway is a 10 kilometer long and winding untarred road, filled with potholes, making it a bumpy ride. Gwali is where I experienced the most devastating trauma of my life. Though I am not a medical practitioner, I do think that it contributed to the onset of mental illness later in my life.

However, Gwali is also where I first witnessed someone else having a mental breakdown and was introduced to the world of mental illness. It was an early Saturday morning, and the sun was already up. The Mabukane household (our home) was abuzz and there were people everywhere. Everybody was getting ready for the afternoon celebrations. This Saturday was all about my grandfather being recognized for dedicating his life to teaching. My grandfather, Lizo Ebenezer Mabukane, had clocked the milestone of 50 years of teaching. My grandmother, Singiswa Louisa Mabukane, was there to support him every step of the way. My mom, Nomathemba Mazaleni, along with my aunts and uncles could not contain their excitement over the fact that there would be all-day festivities in his honour. The children were explicitly told to keep their clothes clean when playing outside, and to remember that the photograper would be taking pictures.

The celebration took place at the only hall in our village and my grandfather appreciated all the effort, especially from his children who had organized the party. Each speaker praised my grandfather for his ongoing dedication to education, and how wonderful it was to see some of his former students go on to make something of themselves - something not easily done in apartheid-era South Africa. One of the many people who were taught by my grandfather, was the late Premier of the Eastern Cape Province, and a former Minister of Sports and Recreation - Makhenkesi Stofile. Even the late Chief Zilimbola Burns-Ncamashe was there to praise my grandfather for his years of contribution to education. My grandfather also made a speech thanking everyone. One of the things he said, was that, were it not for the support of his family, especially my grandmother, it would have been exceedingly difficult for him to find his passion, the way he did in teaching.

At 13:00, people were directed to meet at the Mabukane residence to enjoy lunch. My grandma had cooked up a storm and my mom and my aunts had made different salad dishes. The people from the hall came back to the house and despite the busyness, we managed to have lunch. The photographer who was

TO INSANITY AND BEYOND

hired for the day, took the most beautiful pictures, and captured the essence of the celebration. My favourite pictures to this day, are all the family portraits. After lunch, the adults started to drink. The real party was about to start- and so was the madness. The music started, and people danced with abandon. It was such a happy occasion, and everyone was having a wonderful time.

I was seven years old. As a child I could not make sense of the excessive drinking and laughter and most notably the change in adult behavior which resulted. People were enjoying themselves; some would get up and dance while the rest of the people opted to stay seated and enjoy the loud conversation. The higher the voices, the lower the drinks became and although it was an entertaining get-together and celebration, it somehow got out of hand because of the drinking. The farewell party for my grandfather turned into a real drunk fest as people were really digging into the alcohol. As the drinking escalated, so too did what sounded like an argument.

While observing the general chaos, I saw my aunt *Thandi, suddenly bolt out of the house, running for dear life. My aunt seemed intoxicated, but her steps were faster and faster by the second. As her pace increased, so too did that of the men chasing after her. They chased her, hot on her trail. Even though she knew she was being chased, she was not slowing down. She ran so fast until she reached a cave-like ditch by the side of the road, she jumped into it, and claimed the cave as hers. When the men finally caught up with her, she refused to come out. Inside this ditch she was yelling, crying, singing and shouting at whoever tried to approach her ditch.

People congregated around the ditch and were talking to her, and they urged her to make her way up to them. After a couple of hours, she finally lifted herself up and it was then that the men who had been chasing her, jumped on her, tackled her to the ground, and all you could hear was her shouting, screaming, and crying. She was visibly in distress as the men were tying a rope around her ankles, including her arms and the general body area. The whole thing was bizarre to watch, and I felt so sorry for my aunt especially since she seemed to have no control over what was happening to her.

According to the family, my aunt was having a nervous breakdown and there was no further explanation given. I had no clue what a nervous breakdown meant. I thought she needed medical attention and the fact that she was tied up in a rope did not help my confusion. What was happening at the time was difficult to comprehend and my aunt had no clue about how serious her situation was, but the nurses in the family, including my mother, were quick to point out that she was having a breakdown and she needed to be hospitalized. They were overruled and instead my aunt was taken home so that she could calm down without the noise of the party affecting her recovery. Unfortunately, she was left tied up which was something I found difficult to make sense of. The fact that she was restrained seemed a bit inhumane to me as a child. Yes, she was intoxicated, but there was something more than just the effects of the alcohol at work and it wasn't hard to conclude that she needed medical attention. I cannot imagine how she must have felt or what thoughts were going through her mind. Looking back now, it seems clear to me that she was also struggling with a mental disorder. To me, it seems more likely that she had some form of depression or schizophrenia or maybe even bipolar disorder, rather than it just being an alcohol induced rage. That would explain why she looked and sounded so weird and wild.

I was utterly confused about everything that was taking place and the adults were not forthcoming about what was going on. So, it was up to me to draw my own conclusions. Later in life, I learned that when someone is having a mental breakdown, they tend to have either extremely low or high energy levels. In my aunt's case the energy levels were out of this world. It is worth mentioning, that often when a person is suffering from one form of mental illness or another, it is common to deal with things such as impulsivity, increased sex drive, poor decision making, impulsive rage, paranoia, psychotic episodes, lack of sleep, aggression, tunnel vision, risky behaviour and a tendency to become extremely emotional. That was my aunt.

Watching my aunt being manic and man-handled was a terrible experience. Yes, times have changed, and we have a better understanding and awareness of those with mental health issues, but what is vital to remember, is to treat people with mental health issues with dignity and kindness. I am extremely optimistic that the treatment and care of people surviving and living with mental illness is already evolving and people will receive the care they deserve.

I just want to take a moment to say, that when dealing with someone with mental illness, it is important to be alert and to watch out for triggers. Triggers can be anything, but in essence they are what can begin a mental health episode. When a person is struggling with a mental illness, it is particularly important to look for the underlying causes; such as trauma, because these could shed light on where things went wrong and provide clues to what is and isn't a trigger. It is also important to be vigilant and to take note of behaviours that seem out of the 'normal'.

Anyway, back to our story, these were the turbulent times I grew up in when I was living in Mdantsane. When Siyasanga and I were sent to live with our grandparents, I was devasted, mostly because I wanted to stay in my home, with my parents. Little did I know that great harm awaited me, and I could not have imagined the extent of the trauma which lay ahead. Mdantsane was going up in flames. Riots were taking place, there were school uprisings and there was boycotting of shops, which resulted in so much looting. So, my parents sent us to Gwali to be safe. Out of the frying pan into the fire they say. Living with my grandparents was fun in the beginning, but I realize now that Gwali was a terrible place to raise a girl child. Although my grandparents' home was full of love, patience and understanding, it was just not enough, especially if one considers what I endured, for it was in Gwali that I was raped as a child.

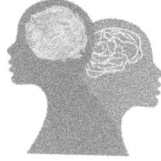

CHAPTER 2

Open Secret

"Life is an open secret. Everything is available, nothing is hidden. All that you need is just eyes to see." ~ **Osho**

Soon after we arrived, life in Gwali seemed to have settled as we followed a routine, and my grandparents were more than happy to have us around. My grandad went back to teaching after his retirement and my grandma took care of us. It was not difficult for Siyasanga and I to acclimatize to Gwali as we were accustomed to going to our grandparents' for holidays. The school we went to, was a big mud house divided according to the different grades. The school was without a doubt a downgrade compared to my former township school in Mdantsane. I was excited to start grade 1 and even though I did not have friends yet, I was optimistic that things would turn out ok. It was delightful to be back in Gwali and even though the standard of living was a bit low in Alice, my grandma made up for it with her cooking - which was out of this world delicious!

My favorite part about school was when we would go home at break time. We would be welcomed by a warm home-cooked meal and my grandma's reassurance that we are going to be ok if we listened to our teachers. Siya and I would literally run home because we would be excited about what we were having for lunch. The fact that my grandma was uneducated didn't deter her from being passionate about education. She never shied away from giving us advise or some words of wisdom. Though I missed my parents very much, I felt happy living with my grandparents. My granddad came out of retirement to become the principal of the school, and he always encouraged us to do better at school and outside of school.

Everything was going well until...

His name was Mvuleni, he was a neighbour who must have been in his early 20s. He was always at our house giving my granddad a hand with car issues, on any given day. He was 'trustworthy', polite, and helpful around the house. Of course, later this led me to believe that everything he was doing with my granddad was just a ruse to conceal the pain he was inflicting on me, when no one was looking.

Mvuleni, started sexually abusing me when I was 6 years old. It went on for 2 years without any adult noticing. The whole experience made me feel numb - tears would roll down my face,

27

but no sound came from my mouth. I could not comprehend this kind of violation. The man who raped me had no remorse whatsoever about what he was doing to me. I did not know how to tell an adult because I feared that he might do something violent to me. He continued helping my granddad around the house or with fixing our car which meant that I would see him all the time. I had to pretend that everything was fine, however, I was petrified of him.

Mvuleni was so good at pretending to be just 'the guy next door'. He was charming and a bit of a con-artist. He was friendly with my grandparents but there was always something very shady about him. His power over me ensured that I would tell no one and that his secret was safe. When he was violating me, I could feel his breath on my neck. This brought me to tears but screaming was not an option. When I tried to resist, he would pin me down, increasing his intensity. His hand was on my mouth so that I could not scream, and he continued to violate me in the most barbaric way possible. When he was finished, I would lie there motionless. My private parts and my tiny body were in unbearable pain. I would struggle tremendously to walk which meant that I needed time to compose myself and get rid of the "evidence." Every time he violated me, it was the same ritual. My silent cries were ignored. I often wonder why I never told my grandparents. My only conclusion is that I must have been scared of what Mvuleni might do to me, because he often whispered that he would harm me if I told anyone.

28

Psychologically, I was a mess and I acted out a lot, I was also very moody and snappy with my friends. I had serious anger issues and the smallest thing would set me off. I often wondered why the adults in my family never heard all my silent cries. All I needed was somebody to save me from this monster of a man. Could it be that they could not fathom this level of violation towards a child? Every time I thought it was safe to tell an adult, I would end up thinking about Mvuleni's hand pressed against my mouth. His grip on me was very aggressive and he would threaten me with violence. I did not tell a single soul about my experience - mostly because I did not know how to. As time went by, I was able to suppress this memory as far back as my subconscious would allow. While my emotions were flip flopping, I was desperately trying to soothe the pain. Physically and psychologically I was 'bleeding.' My temperament changed drastically. I went from being a bubbly child to being passive aggressive, then angry, and, then extremely confrontational. I felt a lot of shame, as though I had 'allowed' or consented to the trauma. I was overwhelmed with so much guilt and the question I would repeatedly ask myself, was, "Why me?". For many years, I could not stop the memories from popping up in my head unexpectedly, and when they did, it felt like the walls were closing in on me.

As I mentioned, I really enjoyed my grandmother's cooking while living with my grandparents. She cooked various meals, which she must have been cooking from memory because

I never saw any cookbooks in the house. After dinner and soon after listening to the news at 7pm, my grandfather would turn off the radio, this was a ritual every evening. As children, we were required to get up and stand by the door and start reciting Bawo Wethu Osemazulwini which is the Lord's Prayer in isiXhosa. Thereafter, my grandfather would pull out The Methodist Church Hymn book. That, and the bible, were in isiXhosa, not English. Next, we sang hymns that granddad would choose, then there would be a scripture reading and lastly, a prayer session- usually done by my grandmother. Even though we had been doing this ritual for many years it was all confusing for me. On the one hand my family was religious, to a point that my granddad was one of the deacons at church. However, as Xhosa people, we still practiced traditional rituals and these rituals meant that we were in tune with our ancestors and whatever messages they may bring in our lives. Though we did this ritual whenever we were with my grandparents, I could never reconcile tradition with religion. I just decided that it was up to the adults to educate me on how to balance the two. To me, it simply felt like I should follow whatever direction the adults were giving me, with no questions, because of course, "God and the ancestors do not like to be questioned." And yet, I had a lot of questions I wanted to ask though this was discouraged. I figured that it would make sense when I too became an adult.

It didn't.

After so many unanswered questions in my life, I made the choice to live my life as an atheist. Neither God nor the ancestors were, able to protect a child from a rapist, so of what use are they?

After 2 years of rape, Siya and I moved back to Mdantsane with my mom and dad. Despite the ongoing riots and the looting that was taking place in the township, my parents felt that it was safe enough to come back and live with them. As soon as we were settled, I received the most devastating news. My mom and dad were getting divorced, and my mom would have custody of Siya and I. This really affected me, as a result I could not figure out if the divorce had something to do with me or not. I honestly thought that I was somehow responsible for what was happening to my parents.

It is amazing how children tend to carry the burdens of their parents.

After my mom left the marital home, we moved around a bit until we settled in a township called Gompo. This was a new development created for civil servants. The area we moved to was nice and modern and there were lots of children to play with. My mom knew a few people in Gompo and some of them were her friends from Mdantsane. At first, I was skeptical about moving, but then it seemed like we were going to be happy in this new neighbourhood. Our favourite part was the small park at the bottom of the houses where we used to play. More importantly, there was no Mvuleni there to rape me.

By 1993 I was 13 years old, and I was doing Standard 6 at Alphandale Secondary School. This is where I realized just how much I loved History as a subject. Granted, we were not taught South African history due to the political climate in the country at the time, but we were taught European History. My favorite period was the Renaissance. This period made me curious and left me wanting to learn more.

Midway through Standard 6, I started hanging out with a boy who was 3 years my senior, and who attended the same high school I did. Walking home from school one day, he suggested that we pass by his house to pick something up. When we got to his house there was no one home. He invited me in and directed me to his bedroom. From his behaviour, it became obvious that he wanted to have sex with me. Realizing this I started to scream, but he put his hand over my mouth. At that moment, I could not believe that this was going to happen, again! I cried as he forced himself on me. I wanted to push him, but I was pinned down with one arm, while his other hand still covered my mouth. It must have been 10 minutes of scuffling with him and me trying to defend myself before he gained an advantage over me and was able to do what he had set out to do.

He raped me.

It felt like forever. The sexual assault continued until we started hearing voices in the house which it turned out to be his mother and sister. When he was done, I just sat there motionless with warm tears running down my cheeks. The look of panic on his face showed that he was in trouble. We stayed in his bedroom for a while until he felt sure about walking me out. We walked past the bathroom, into the kitchen, and out of the door without being seen by his mother or sister who were sitting in the lounge area. I never spoke to him again. When I saw him at school, I simply ignored him. I didn't know what else to do.

Bizarrely, the boy who raped me at 13 went on to become an adult who now works for the South African Police Service (SAPS). It makes me wonder if he ever deals with rape cases at work and if so, what's his reaction to such cases? I also find it ironic that a person who was a rapist himself, can now deal with offenders from a place of authority. I struggle to reconcile how someone with a career in SAPS can have such a dark past and can just go on with life as if he were never guilty of sexual assault. In simple terms, this man is making a mockery of the Justice System. I cannot help thinking that if his employers were to find out about this transgression, would he would be out of a job? Has he raped anyone else? Does he use his position as a police officer to rape with impunity now?

I have since made peace with this trauma, found some healing, but that did not stop the memories from haunting me. It is because of these experiences and the trauma I experienced at the hands of those two men, that my relationship with men has become distorted.

The first time I attempted suicide I was 16 years old and doing Std. 7 at the time. I took a bunch of pills from the house and as much as I knew that the pills may cause damage, I still took them. No one knew what I was up to, so I took advantage of the fact that no one was paying attention. I had cramps, I was sweating, vomiting and I struggled to stand up straight. The funny thing was that when I started vomiting my mother started to become more alert and I suspected that she thought I was pregnant. I did not tell my mom what the real issue was and at the time I did not know anything about being depressed. All I knew, was that "stress is dangerous" and it can have serious implications on one's general health - and I was always stressed.

I changed schools a lot in my teens. This was a challenge because I did not stay in one school long enough to make any real friends. The suicide attempt happened when I was doing Standard 7 and even though I knew why I was vomiting so much I could not bring myself to confess to my mom what I had done. I was terrified of telling anyone about this. I did not even tell Siya who already suspected that something was peculiar about my behaviour. I was so clueless about a lot of things, especially issues related to mental health, but I knew a lot about feeling empty, feeling lost, and about perpetual pain. I cried all the time. All this drama and trauma made me feel trapped and all the skeletons which haunted me seemed intent on dragging me down the rabbit hole.

34

The year I turned 17, my mom told me she booked me a ticket to fly to Argentina to visit her uncle, the late Ambassador Aubrey Nkomo, an anti-apartheid stalwart. He had invited me to go to Argentina to visit him and his wife Barbara Nkomo and this would take place in December of 1997. I spent most of that year extremely excited about the trip and it got even more exciting because after Argentina I would get to visit my mom's friend and colleague based in Boston, USA - Pat Meservey. I had not met Aunty Pat at all growing up, but when I saw her at the airport, I felt like I knew her already. The trip to North and South America was going to be epic. Just before the trip, I really struggled to sleep at night or focus on anything else because I just wanted the time to pass quickly. The countries I was going to visit were total opposites especially where weather was concerned. It was summer in Buenos Aires which was the same as South African weather and Boston was in the middle of winter with lots of snow. Either way this was one of the best experiences to ever happen to me. I could not contain my excitement and rightly so, because this was big, I mean, coming from the township and being given an opportunity to go overseas for two months and travelling alone was simply the best. I am utterly grateful to my mom for having given me that opportunity.

I arrived in Buenos Aires on a Wednesday, and I was picked up from the airport by my uncle's driver who could not really speak English, so our communication was stunted. The driver brought me to a massive apartment complex and their home was at the top of this building. When I arrived, my uncle was still at work, so I was introduced to the two ladies who were responsible for the housekeeping. That first day was quite a challenge, because the two ladies could not speak a single word of English and I could not speak a word of Spanish. They were speaking with me in Spanish, I responded in English and there was also a bit of sign language, but it just went downhill from there. The language barrier proved to be challenging, very challenging, particularly when it was time to ask for food. I was feeling nervous already and I could not wait for my uncle to finish work.

Argentina was amazing, and so was my uncle. We even went to a James Brown concert which was super cool. We took a big boat to the neighbouring country of Uruguay - which is only a boat ride away across the River Plate. I got to visit the area where Tango dance started. It was also fascinating to see such a rich culture, good food, and entertainment and most notably the Argentineans were very friendly. I spent Christmas in Argentina and New Year's in Boston. I also had a wonderful time in Boston with Aunty Pat and her family. I have been extremely fortunate to have a mother who supports me the way my mom does, especially when I think about all the opportunities, she has afforded me. But, as great as this trip was, it could not undo the rapes and could not contain the anger building up inside of me. The pain never goes away.

I am incredibly grateful that my family understands my personal history and the connection to my mental health issues now. I have come a long way since I was first diagnosed and over time, I have managed to understand my illness with all its layers and its relationship to my past. My horrible experiences with rape are forever linked to the things which trigger my bipolar disorder. It has been quite a journey, but for some reason I now feel like I am finally in tune with my brain, and as a result I am finally managing to get some balance in my life. If that weren't the case, I would never be able to write about my trauma now.

When I turned 18 years old, that trauma returned as nightmarish memories. This time I decided to not keep quiet about what I was remembering, so I told my mother about my rape experiences. My mother was broken by this confession, she was shocked and sympathetic at the same time. We talked about the psychological effect of these things, and she wanted to find out where I was emotionally, and asked for my permission to look for a psychologist who would help me to put things into perspective. And so, I first entered the world of psychotherapy.

I want to let the reader know that it was a struggle to write this chapter. It may even have been disturbing to read. The idea was mainly to highlight a trauma that has held me ransom for most of my life. It is very important for me to give insights about the correlation between trauma and mental illness. As I was reflecting about some of the things I endured, I realized that it is common for people, particularly black families to **not** talk openly and honestly about issues related to rape. Concealing these things can often mean that the survivor is left hanging. In our communities, to a certain extent, it is uncommon to have healthy conversations about mental health because the topics are considered way too sensitive to talk about. That needs to change. When people who suffer from mental illness feel rejected by society, it is possible that the rejection first originated with their family.

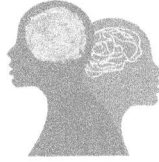

CHAPTER 3

Running to Nowhere

"That's the place to get to—nowhere. One wants to wander away from the world's somewheres, into our own nowhere."
~ *D.H. Lawrence*

In 2003, I turned 23 and was in my third year of study at the University of the Western Cape. This is also the year I fell pregnant with my first child. At the time I was in a relationship, and he was thrilled with the news. So was I. He had no family in Cape Town to worry about or to share the news with. In the Xhosa culture, a man who makes a woman pregnant, is required to pay 'damages' to the family of the woman. However, this practice is based on the idea that two families will come together and will be united for the benefit of the unborn child. Unfortunately, he had no one to help him negotiate or pay for the 'damages' with my uncles. In the beginning of my pregnancy, my mother was surprised and not impressed by the news of my pregnancy, mostly because she was worried that I had not finished with my studies. Late that November I gave birth to my beautiful baby boy, I named him Hope, and his grandma gave him the name Mangaliso after a family friend - the late Doctor Mangaliso Maqhina. Hope was born prematurely by about a month, so he was a tiny baby weighing about 1.8 kg, but after a few weeks, he started to gain weight and six months later he was a healthy and a happy baby. However, I was not doing well. I struggled with my emotions. My moods were frequently going up and down and chronic insomnia meant I got no rest. Also, my relationship with Hope's father deteriorated rapidly during the pregnancy and in short, I became a single parent.

It took a while but eventually, sometime after Hope's arrival in the world, I was diagnosed with Postpartum Depression which is common among women after giving birth. The Mayo Clinic describes postpartum depression as:

"...the baby blues after childbirth, which commonly include mood swings, crying spells, anxiety and difficulty sleeping. Postpartum Depression typically begins within the first two to three days after delivery and may last up to two weeks."

I was in a bad space; every little thing would set me off and I reached a point where I did not know whether I was coming or going. My mother, being a nurse, identified the condition quickly and contacted Dr. Kaplan, my OBGYN who had delivered my baby. He referred me to Dr. Rausch, a psychiatrist who admitted me to Kenilworth Clinic for 'rest'. After I was discharged from the clinic, I still struggled with depression and was given medication to treat it. But medication can be hit or miss when it comes to mental health and in my case, it was a 'miss'.

In February of 2004, I took the very same medication I had been given for my depression and attempted to commit suicide once again. This time I was admitted to Mediclinic Durbanville where they pumped my stomach to flush out all the pills in my system. At the time my mother was based in Boston, MA in the United States of America. She called me every day to check up on me. My mother was grieved to hear that I tried to commit suicide. She did not understand the extent to which my 'demons' were haunting me.

Eventually things settled down for me and for a short time I found that elusive 'balance'. Then at 26, having recently graduated from the University of the Western Cape, I was awarded a scholarship to go and study in The Netherlands. I took up my Master of Science degree at The University of Maastricht's School of Government. I was excited to be accepted to an international program where all the students were from various parts of the world. My mother, who believes in the power of education, encouraged me to go and offered to stay with Hope while I was busy with my studies for that year. One piece of advice my mom gave me was that I should focus on my education and stay away from weed or the 'coffee shops', especially since 'pot' is legal in The Netherlands. Luckily, I was not into marijuana at the time. I came back to South Africa once in that entire year. I took the opportunity to go to Cape Town on a mini holiday with Hope. We had a fantastic time - especially our trips to the beach. We really bonded because we had lots of activities to do together. However, he was not pleased that I would be going back to The Netherlands. It was heartbreaking leaving my baby boy behind.

Back in The Netherlands, I was doing fine until I again started feeling depressed. My depression at this point was crippling, and I couldn't get myself out of bed in the mornings, let alone go to my classes. The one thing that usually gives me some relief when I'm on a downward spiral, is my medication. I saw a doctor for this but it was a struggle to get the medication that would help me with my condition. I can't say enough about how important it is to have medication that is right for you. My situation was not helped by the language barrier, but eventually I was prescribed suitable antidepressants for my depression. Even though I'm familiar with Afrikaans in South Africa, but sadly, I struggled to understand Dutch despite the fact that Afrikaans originates from Dutch. The fact that it proved to be a challenge to get the right medication, I was very relieved to get the medication.

Then one afternoon I was depressed enough that I decided to travel from Maastricht to Amsterdam and visit a travel agency to book a flight to South Africa. I wanted to go home badly. Of course, it was not the best time to travel home, and my scholarship would not approve of my trip, but I still wanted to go. I'm not sure how I made the decision to stay in the Netherlands, but I did. I went back to the train station, feeling overwhelmed, despondent, and anxious, and being back on the platform waiting to board the train, all I was thinking was "don't get too close to the tracks because then you may try to jump". I planted myself firmly by the wall and you would think that this would be a simple task, but I struggled tremendously because of everything that was unraveling in my world. I briefly left the platform to get some fresh air and when I went back, my train was just arriving. I boarded the train, and I was back in Maastricht in my little apartment and very relieved that I was there safely, though I was still annoyed at the thought of not going home.

My studies were quite intense, because what I felt should have been a two-year course was crammed into one year. Still, I was able to manage my depression because the doctor prescribed anti-depressants which lifted my mood and kept me balanced. I am still not sure of how I managed to cope with the workload and the writing of my thesis. At the end of the program, I was pleased, because this meant I would finally go back to South Africa and see my mom and my son. I often reflect on the time I spent at the University of Maastricht, including the friendships I made. I am convinced that that year was so important to my personal growth and so important to learning to live with

CHASING SANITY

depression. Even though I had doubts about seeing the program through, I managed to stick it out, and finish – I persevered. I was over the moon when I was awarded my Master of Science in Public Policy and Human Development certificate.

When I returned to Pretoria mid-2007, I went back to my job at the Department of Water Affairs and Forestry (DWAF). Things kind of got back to normal for me, but I was eager to change jobs, so I started looking for a new job whilst I was at DWAF. I was incredibly lucky, that within two months of looking, there was an opening at a Non-Governmental Organization (NGO) called Institute for Democracy in Southern Africa (IDASA). I was thrilled to get a job at such a reputable organization as IDASA and the fact that several staff members were international, made it even better. Things were really falling into place for me, and I was go, go, go.

In February of 2008, I was out with friends, and we went to a club called Fashion TV in Brooklyn (South Africa) and had so much fun, drinking and dancing. While we were at the club, I met *Ayanda, and we started talking about everything under the sun and it was clear that we had chemistry. Ayanda is Pedi and I am Xhosa, so we spoke English mostly and occasionally we would revert to our own languages. Our languages are very different from each other but I managed to speak Pedi, thanks to the time I spent in Pretoria. He was a smooth talker and it turned out he was single just like I was. We spent a lot of time together going to nice restaurants, relaxing at his house and simply enjoying each other's company.

One night we were chatting. The conversation became deep, especially the part where he wanted to find out what exactly happened to me when I was a child, and although I thought it was a bizarre question, I still shared with him the details of being raped. Ayanda was sympathetic and he comforted me, but soon after he left to go meet his friends. I was then left all alone in his house, thinking non-stop about what I had just told Ayanda and how he felt about me now? The first thing I did was to look for pills to numb the pain. I raided his medicine cabinet and took a handful of pills. I was feeling lethargic and the fact that I didn't care what the pills where for, I took them anyway. Not knowing what the pills were for certainly did not discourage me. I had a plan. I just wanted to be free of the pain. When I started being drowsy, I called Ayanda and told him what I had done, he rushed back and took me to the hospital where I was admitted as a high-risk patient.

It was while I was in hospital that the attending physician and nurse mocked my situation. After checking my file, the white doctor told me that I "…should have simply jumped in front of a moving train because that would have been more effective and quicker than ending up on a hospital bed". So much for the Hippocratic Oath! I could not believe my ears when this was said to me and to make it even worse, the black nurse was agreeing with the white doctor.

I must say, that I come across a lot of people who are ignorant about mental health. They tend to have a lack of understanding, a lack of compassion and a lack of interest in the subject. I just don't expect them to be health professionals. Often, this ignorance manifests as poking fun at the person who is struggling with mental illness. Considering why I was in hospital, it was cruel that a doctor and a nurse of all people, would advise me to go jump in front of a train to commit suicide "properly." Maybe the doctor and nurse may have been trying to dissuade me by showing me some 'tough love' or maybe they were trying to be funny, but whatever it was that they were trying to achieve, they simply came across as very insensitive. The comments made by that doctor were awful. When you become a target for ridicule, it is easy to feel discouraged and despondent. It is no wonder people living with mental illnesses tend to suffer in silence.

For some people it is easy to be open and honest about their illness. For most people it is not easy to share details of their mental health, for fear of being judged or treated differently. The stigma attached to mental illness which people like me endure starts with jokes, but before you know it, it seems like the comic relief is always at your expense. The worst way to offend someone who is surviving mental illness is to belittle them or call them derogatory names. The best way to deal with those of us who have mental illness, is to grasp that we need respect, understanding, compassion, kindness, and most importantly we need help.

Ayanda and I were supposed to celebrate his birthday in March, and I planned a bit of an elaborate celebration for just the two of us. I made reservations at the fancy Palazzo Montecasino Hotel in Fourways. This meant I would have to drive from Pretoria to Midrand, which was a little over 30km and then Ayanda and I would take one car to Fourways. I got on the N1 and about 15 minutes into the drive I realized that there was an annoying noise coming from the back of the car. Before I was able to reach the closest petrol station, I stopped by the side of the road and confirmed that the noise was coming from a puncture. I called Ayanda, and I told him what happened. He came to help me with one of his friends, *Malusi. When they arrived it was already dark, though it was only 7pm. The N1 was busy as usual but there was nothing sinister about the evening. Ayanda and Malusi removed the damaged tyre and replaced it with the spare. As soon as they were finished with the tyre situation, we saw four men emerging from the bushes and coming towards my car. The men pulled out guns and forced us into the car. The hijackers tried to put Ayanda and Malusi in the boot, but they soon realized that it would be impossible due to the limited space in the Jeep. This worked in our favour. Ayanda and Malusi were then pushed and shoved into the middle of the backseat. On either side of them there were guys pointing guns at them. I sat in the front passenger seat and next to me was another guy also pointing a gun at me. He was extremely aggressive. I was terrified for my life, especially when he started shouting in a language I could not understand. He was groping and touching me inappropriately. I was so sure that they were going to rape me. In the driver's seat sat one of the hijackers, with a gun pointed at me like he was going to pull the trigger.

The ordeal must have lasted twenty minutes to half an hour, but it felt much longer. We were lucky to come out of it without any scratches. They let us go because Ayanda had a lot of cash in his car and gave it to them. They took it and ran off into the night. We had just literally 'dodged a bullet'. I cancelled the dinner reservation because we were too distraught. We spent the next couple of hours going to two different police stations. At the first police station, we were told that where the crime took place wasn't their jurisdiction, and therefore we needed to report the crime at Midrand police station. At the Midrand police station, two of the of the hijackers were already in custody. We were lucky because those vile men did not take us to a secluded place to rape me or worse, kill us. Since that evening, I made the decision that if I could, I was not going to raise my child in South Africa. I wanted to leave and go to a place where I did not have to worry about my safety and that of my family.

The second part of 2008 was very chaotic but also filled with opportunities. I was promoted at IDASA from Personal Assistant at States in Transition Observatory (SITO) to Junior

Researcher with the Aids Budget Unit. I was incredibly pleased by the promotion. While I was with the Aids Budget Unit, I was awarded a placement with the MAC Aids Fund Leadership Initiative. The MAC AIDS Fund Leadership Initiative was established by MAC cosmetics in partnership with UCLA Program in Global Health and Columbia University's HIV Center for Clinical and Behavioural Studies. Essentially, MAC cosmetics used their Viva Glam Lipstick as a campaign for raising awareness about HIV/AIDS. All the proceeds from the Viva Glam Lipstic went towards HIV/AIDS research.

MAC AIDS Fund Leadership Initiative was also designed to support HIV/AIDS projects across the globe, and especially in developing countries. Being part of this prestigious program meant that I would go for almost two months of training with UCLA in Global Health and this was held in Johannesburg. Thereafter I would go for another two months to the United States of America and get further training at Columbia University in New York. This was a collaboration between Mailman School of Public Health and the HIV Center for Clinical and Behavioural Studies. This opportunity meant that I would have two jobs, one with IDASA and the other one with the Mac Aids Fund Leadership Initiative. However, at IDASA, I would take a leave without pay and my position would be frozen. Out of hundreds who applied, the program only accepted 8 candidates, I was ecstatic about being chosen as one of the candidates who would go to New York. Life was good.

Fast forward to our arrival in New York, we were picked up at JFK International Airport by two directors of the program. We were told that we would be based in Hoboken New Jersey, and commute back and forth between Manhattan and Hoboken. We were given Metro cards that we would use when commuting. New York City is so big, with so many skyscrapers and massive billboards, no wonder we were captivated. Columbia University is located on the Upper Westside of Manhattan which meant that we would not have to walk too far to catch the train. My colleagues and I worked extremely hard, from attending seminars to doing presentations. All of them were highly informative regarding the major topic of HIV/AIDS.

The idea was that, while we were attending the workshops, we would simultaneously work on our individual projects. Thereafter, we would present our projects to the Director and our colleagues. The job was very demanding, and rewarding at the same time. Waking up every morning to cross the Hudson River was taking a toll on me though. In Hoboken, we were all sharing the apartments, which meant that we were sharing with one extra person per apartment and *my* house mate was *Ashley. During the week we worked extremely hard, and on the weekends, we played even harder.

Ashely had a cousin who lived in New York and we would often meet up with him when he was done with work. One time we went to a Music Festival in Coney Island, where everyone dressed up in different and elaborate outfits. The outfits, the music and the vibe reminded me of Burning Man. A few months before I left South Africa for New York, I was experimenting with hard drugs, and cocaine became my drug of choice. In the beginning, I was taking it recreationally, but it escalated to every weekend when I was not working. The fact that I was in a foreign country should have been a deterrence for me, but instead, on the weekends, I would go to parties or meet friends at the bar, and we would drink alcohol. When there was no booze we did cocaine, then we would smoke marijuana if we didn't have access to cocaine. We would snort this white powder until we could not remember our own names. The drugs take a toll on your body. The drugs mess with your mind and it can feel like you have been hit by a bus, especially if you have an undiagnosed mental illness as well. If you are struggling with depression, as I do, taking drugs meant that I was straining my body and my brain. It was common that after a big night out I would sleep for 24 hours straight and wake up feeling like I could go on sleeping for another 24 hours, which was not good for studying.

Coming back home to South Africa, I continued with partying and doing drugs with my friends in Johannesburg. I did not realize that I went from recreationally taking drugs to becoming an addict. I did not think of myself as an addict, largely because the times I used drugs were infrequent as far as I was concerned, but I was fully committed to them when I did partake. It was quite a rollercoaster and for a while it felt like I was stuck in darkness, and it is through this darkness that I found my light and I eventually quit drugs and I have never looked back. What also helped was moving away from the drug life in Johannesburg to settle in Hout Bay, Cape Town because this required a total mind shift. I left the big city for a sleepy village.

So, there you have it. I had to dig deep to let my skeletons out of the closet from this time of my life. My on-and-off struggles with depression, more trauma and the drug use were difficult to endure but I also had a pretty good life going on. I just don't want these things in my past to own me anymore, so I need to be open about them.

I do, however, want to say that I know that trauma is not always linked to mental illness. But there is an undeniable correlation between trauma and mental illness. Saprea, a nonprofit organization focused on eliminating child sexual abuse, tells us that "...85% of child sexual abuse survivors experience at least one diagnosable mental health disorder by age 30". My former psychologist in Cape Town used to encourage me to deal with my trauma head-on. She would highlight trusting the process of healing. Although the journey to my healing may seem hard, long and winding, the progress I have made over the years leads me to believe that this journey is worth it. I keep reminding myself how far I have come and how far I'm still going to go.

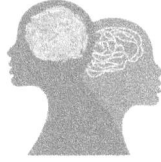

CHAPTER 4

The Calm Before the Storm

"I am not only the calm before the storm, I am both the calm and storm." ~**Ivy Atalanta**

Hout Bay is known for being 'a drinking village with a fishing problem'. It's a beautiful seaside village on the Cape Peninsula with three access points, guarded by tall mountains. The first access point is over Constantia Nek, which leads to False Bay. The second entry point is down Suikerbossie which leads back to Cape Town. This route has the most amazing view of Hout Bay beach and views of the big boats docked at the harbour. But the last route takes the cake; this picturesque route from the famous Chapman's Peak side is where you can see Hout Bay laid out like a beautiful quilt. Driving from Chapman's Peak, one is guaranteed to enjoy the view of distinct peaks like the Sentinel and Karbonkelberg, and from this drive one gets to see all of Hout

Bay. This place has some of the most exquisite houses. The property market is popular among foreigners, but way too expensive for most locals. This is also apparent when you look at the layout of the town. As beautiful as Hout Bay is, it is one of the few places in Cape Town where the gap between the haves and have-nots feels wider and more in your face. For a small community it is distinctly segregated. There are areas where you find nice, luxurious houses, occupied by mostly White people and a few wealthy Black people. Then, there are the two townships. Hangberg, which is occupied by mostly poor Coloured people; fishermen, smugglers, and their families- and Imizamo Yethu which is occupied by poor black people.

I first moved to Hout Bay from Newlands in 2004. In Newlands I lived with Hope, Thuli and Siya for a year until we moved to Hout Bay. The place we shared in Newlands was very central, diverse and close to the University of Cape Town. We were located on the Main Road and in close proximity to South African Breweries (SAB). On any given day, your senses could be assaulted by the foul smell of beer being brewed at SAB. At the time, my mom transferred to the U.S. for work. She had just purchased a new home in Hout Bay so Siya, Thulisa, Hope and I moved there. Soon after, Hope and I moved to Pretoria for my new job with the Department of Water Affairs and Forestry. In 2010, I came full circle, I moved back to the Bay, looking for a new job and a more stress-free life.

My first stay in Hout Bay left a great impression on me. I wanted to raise Hope in a hassle-free environment and this tranquil place fit that description. It's a melting pot of different people, cultures, and food. This diversity goes a long way to ensuring inclusivity, despite the obvious barriers between races and wealth. My favourite thing about Hout Bay, though, is the real sense of community spirit. Add to that, the uncommon beauty of the bay and it felt like home.

Hout Bay has a sizeable number of restaurants, but my favourite is Pakalolo. This turned out to be the place where I met my husband, Fin. It was mid-March 2011, and it was my friend Jenna's birthday. We decided to go to Pakalolo for birthday drinks. It was voting season in South Africa, so when we joined a group of friends it was not a major surprise that we were talking about all thing's election. The drinks were flowing and so was the conversation. While we were chatting, a member of the group, returned from the washroom. I was immediately taken by him. My first words to him were, "Hey big fellow what's your story?" From there we started talking. I introduced myself and I found out that he was a Canadian named was Fin, and he worked as a Sailing Instructor at the V&A Waterfront. Soon after our chat he left, but we exchanged numbers and said we would go for a drink later that week. He never called me that week, but I did bump into him at Pakalolo again and gave him a cold shoulder. Fin asked me for my cell number again, I was annoyed. I was certain that I had given him my number when we met the first time. I grabbed his phone, scrolled through his contacts, found my name, and showed it to him. He was surprised that he had saved my number but then forgotten to call. To make up for the confusion, he asked me out on a date, and I agreed.

Our first date was at a seaside restaurant called Dunes, and I was pleased to see that the restaurant was not full. We had a quiet evening with minimal interruptions between our meals. Midway through our meal, Fin broke out into a sweat and the more he wiped it off the more he was sweating. He was clearly having an allergic reaction to something, but we were not sure if it was from the food or the bottle of wine we were sharing. Apart form being too nervous, it turned out to be the wine that gave Fin an allergic reaction. We had a lovely time getting to know each other and it was genuinely nice to listen to the waves in the background. The food was great, the conversation was uplifting, and it felt like we knew each other very well. Even though Fin sweated buckets on our first date, the most memorable thing about that night was the conversation. We went on a few more dates after that first dinner, and it became clear that we were now an item. It felt like we had a real connection. He was kind and easy to talk to. I also found out that he was 12 years older than me, but this was in no way a deterrent, I already liked him, and I was looking forward to spending more time with him. I should also mention that he is white.

By May, after a mechanical issue with a prophylactic, we found out to our surprise that we were pregnant. We were in love and decided to go for it and have a baby. We were very excited, but that was soon overshadowed by the fact that my gynecologist, Dr. Kaplan, diagnosed me with Placenta Previa. This means that my placenta was lying unusually low in my uterus, and it was covering my cervix. This also meant that I was bleeding as though I were on my period. Dr Kaplan prescribed bed rest so Fin found us a small apartment where we could live together while we planned for the future. Eventually he found a small house with a granny flat for my mother, and just like that we were a family- though it took my mother a while to get used to a large *mlungu* wondering around the place! In isiXhosa, Mlungu is basically a noun used to describe a white person.

I was immobile for a good 4 months. The bed was elevated from the bottom to help with the occasional bleeding, which was terrifying for both Fin and I. I hated being cooped up in the house all the time and even missed being at work. At the time I was working for Fairtrade Label South Africa. It was not easy, but my boss was very understanding and gave me leave without pay. Then, to make matters worse, when I was around 6 months pregnant, Dr. Kaplan did an ultrasound on me. We found out that the baby was in breach. This meant that the baby was lying sideways in my belly, not a good position for delivery, but at least I was scheduled to have a Caesarian Section. But, apart from all the complications, I had a good pregnancy and, on South

Africa's Day of Reconciliation - December 16th, a month premature, our baby entered the world. He was tiny, but he was healthy, and we named him Michael Aidan Lizo. Little Aidan had to stay in Neonatal Care for about 4 days to ensure that his lungs were fully developed. I would visit him and watch him sleep and I could not believe just how much love I had for this tiny person.

Meanwhile the relationship with Fin and my son Hope was growing stronger. He really stepped up to be a good father to Hope and he was hands-on with both our boys - especially Hope. When Hope turned 8 years old in 2011, we threw him a big birthday party, and he had a blast with his friends.

The following year we had two major milestones. One was my mother's 60th birthday party in June, and the second one was our wedding in November. As early as February I started planning our wedding and it always cracks me up to think that Fin was reluctant to get married. Fin's hesitance towards marriage stemmed from the fact that he had been married before and things didn't work out. Despite the fact that I too have been married, I was not discouraged. I had one thing on my mind, and that was to marry this amazing man - so he had no choice. We had my mom's birthday at Tarragona Lodge. It was an intimate celebration with only a few of our friends and family. Unfortunately, Fin could not attend my mom's birthday because he was recovering from pneumonia.

The funny thing is that I never suffered from post-partum depression after Aidan was born, certainly not the way I had after Hope's birth. To be honest I never even thought about it, which may sound strange, but I was just so happy at the time. When I was pregnant with Aidan, I struggled with the idea of Placenta Previa. I had never heard of this term before, and it was a challenge for both Fin and me as we constantly worried about whether I'd carry the baby. Even though we were happy that we were having a baby, at the back of our minds there was this nagging feeling that something could go wrong. So, when he was born and we knew he was healthy, it was all a huge relief.

Fin and I had a civil ceremony on October 18th at the Department of Home Affairs and then on November 17th we had our 'white wedding' at The Twelve Apostles Hotel along the Atlantic Seaboard. It was a lavish affair attended by our local friends -and those who came from overseas - by family, including Fin's dad, his dad's wife and his younger brother, James and sister, Alex. The wedding venue was breathtaking, with the backdrop of the Twelve Apostle Mountains behind the hotel and the front of the hotel overlooking Llandudno Beach. It was exciting to see people I had not seen in a while. The crew from Top Billing was also there to film the wedding including the interview they did with us. The Footage would be broadcast on SABC3 in the next few weeks. Top Billing was a South Afican lifestyle television programme which covered various topics ranging from travel, interiour design, entertainment, weddings etc. My uncle Mthuthuzeli Mabukane walked me down the aisle, while my family and friends sang isiXhosa songs which is common at African weddings. I was pleased to see everyone was in high spirits. We exchanged vows with Richard Smith, Fin's friend, guiding us. Our guests had a fantastic time and so did we. I was on top of the world!

In 2013, we attended two weddings abroad, the first one was Fin's sister. Alex was getting married in Canada, in the Summertime. The second wedding was Fin's cousin Fergus, getting married in Ireland in the Spring. I travelled ahead to Canada with the boys, and we were joined by Fin after he had finished a boat delivery. It was a bit of a mission especially since we had an 8-hour layover at Heathrow Airport in England. The worst part was that Aidan was not well. He threw up all over me and himself, he had a temperature and to make matters worse, we weren't sure if what he ate gave him a tummy ache. Luckily, we had just started boarding the plane, so I had a bit of time to clean him up and change the top I was wearing. Fin arrived in Canada from Morocco about three days before us. Fin was delivering a boat from Cape Town to Gibraltar, he connected via Morocco, and flew to Toronto. My mom, who was also going to be attending the wedding, arrived two days before we did. The wedding at the family farm was exquisite and everyone had a wonderful time. It was during the Canadian wedding that I got to meet Fin's family members and I instantly liked them.

Just before the Ireland trip, we found out that we were pregnant with twins. Unfortunately, after two months I miscarried. I lost the first baby and my gynecologist told me that it was highly unlikely that the second baby would survive, so I played the waiting game. In two or three weeks that followed, I lost the second twin. I could not believe that this was happening. As if that were not enough, I had to go into the hospital for what doctors call the 'Evacuation of the Uterus'.

I was extremely excited to go to Ireland. I was to attend Fergus's wedding. I was mesmerized by the rich culture and food. The good thing was that as a South African I did not need a visa to enter Ireland. We arrived in Dublin and took a bus to the 'real' Bantry Bay (there's a Bantry Bay in Cape Town) where we were picked up by my father-in-law and brother-in-law and proceeded to go to Dunmanus Bay where the family home is located.

I vividly remember being wheeled on a stretcher on my way to the operation room and thinking, 'This is it, there is no going back'! As my tears started to stream down my cheeks, I asked myself how I was going to recover from this. This was one of the most devastating experiences that I have ever gone through. - There seemed to be no rationale to what was happening to my body.

Without a doubt 2013 was just a hot mess, and as I struggled with my emotions and just how heartbroken I was in general; I was on that dark emotional rollercoaster again. There seemed to be no rhyme or reason as to why everything was happening the way it did. What was happening was beyond comprehension. Since I am already prone to depression, it did not take long to see that I was a basket case. It was plain to see that, psychologically, I was taking a pounding and I was not in a space to contend with all this. Quite frankly, I thought all this was so bizarre.

After this traumatic experience, I found myself questioning a lot of things including my religion, my ancestors and God in general. Was He judging me? I certainly had friends and family who made me feel that way. Having to carry a life (or lives) inside your body is quite an extraordinary experience and then to be told that the babies will not survive is just cruel and makes no sense. Why would God do this to me? I cried so much; I was such an emotional wreck. I struggled to make sense of life. On one hand so many people were telling me it was God's will, or worse, that I was being punished. On the other hand, I had Fin, who quietly told me it was not my fault, that it was nature being nature, and that miscarriages are not as uncommon as people think. Eventually, I made the decision to turn my back on Christianity and anything that had to do with God. It was like leaving a bad relationship, one I had been living in forever. At this point I became an Atheist. It has been 8 years since I chose this path, and I have not looked back.

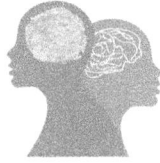

CHAPTER 5

My Storm: The Soundtrack to My Madness

"...I used to bite my tongue and hold my breath. Scared to rock the boat and make a mess. So, I sat quietly, agreed politely. I guess that I forgot I had a chance. I let you push me past the breaking point. I stood for nothing, so I fell for everything. I got the eye of the tiger. Dancing through the fire. Cause I am a champion, and you're gonna hear me roar. Louder, louder than a lion. Cause I am a champion, and you're gonna hear me roar..." ~ **Katy Perry, "Roar"**

I played Katy Perry's Roar non stop in December of 2013. It was my theme song through an extremely difficult period in my life. In fact, this song became the theme song to my mania. Although certain things seemed distorted but what was clear to me is that I was entering unfamiliar territory and sadly I was ill prepared for what lied ahead. It was not hard for me to understand that every time I listened to it, it seemed like the song was fueling my psychosis. Without a doubt, Roar was the soundtrack to my madness. As much as I tried to conceal what was 'brewing' in my brain the weirder everything became. Even more alarming, everything about my behaviour was not adding up.

In the Summer of 2013, I was diagnosed with Bipolar Type 1 Disorder. It was devastating, not least of all because I had to be hospitalized at Somerset Hospital's Psychiatric ward in Cape Town over Christmas. Prior to the diagnosis, I exhibited all the symptoms of being *hypomanic* (one step below mania). I was talking non stop but I wasn't making any sense, there was neither filter no logic in what I was trying to articulate. All kinds of thoughts entered my brain and it was an uphill battle to filter between what was reality and nonsense. Being delusional, passive aggressive, emotional, is just the nature of the beast.

Without a diagnosis from a doctor or psychiatrist, there was not much that I or anyone else could do. I had no idea what was happening in my brain, so I just continued with my life without thinking that there might be something sinister brewing. However, my moods were doing summersaults, I was up then down. I had extreme highs and extreme lows and my energy levels were boundless - interspersed only by sudden crashes where I would sleep for an entire day. I struggled so much with my emotions, and I could not make sense of why there was such a contrast in my moods.

I was emotional all the time without understanding why. I tried my best to be 'normal', but being 'normal' proved to be a challenge. What is 'normal' anyway? A few months before Summer, I was unusually happy most of the time, but who questions being 'happy'? This happiness was often interrupted with bouts of irritability with anyone who threatened my good mood. Often, I would become overly aggressive, getting into conflicts with people close to me. But the overall feeling was that I was on top of the world, however this translated as the mania that was brewing in my brain.

I was also drinking too much. I drank with friends, and when I was by myself, I would drink even more. It was not unusual for me to go to bed anytime between 02:00am and 04:00am, completely drunk, with my brain playing tricks on me.

I had grandiose ideas about anything that crossed my mind. I was constantly writing notes in my journal, but it was the big and small ideas that kept on getting in the way of my sleep. In the middle of the night, when I was drunk, I would call friends and family - especially those who lived overseas - because the time difference was simply perfect for a chat.

Soon after Aidan's second birthday I planned an event where I invited a few of my friends and other business people for the launch of my new media company. I had this little get together at Tarragona Lodge - where we had celebrated my mom's sixtieth. It was well attended by my friends, but the only problem

65

was that there was no rhyme nor reason to the occasion and, as it turned out, I was in a very heightened hypomanic state. I was running around organizing everything, but nothing made sense. Before the event, I went to Woolworths on a serious shopping spree, buying everything I thought I needed to spice up the decorations at Tarragona Lodge. The owner of the Lodge was very patient in the beginning but after a while she lost it when she realized that I was moving the furniture around. Re-arranging spaces and spending loads of money, proved to be another feature of my hypomania. The owner of the lodge did eventually calm down and her only request was that the furniture be moved back to their original spaces. For lunch we had food delivered from Spiros' restaurant and we had great fun, but sadly no one knew what was going on with me. Later, people started leaving and it was not hard to see the look of confusion on their faces. This was the point I began transitioning from hypomania to full mania. As the mania started to kick-in, the whole evening went from being a drama to a tragicomedy.

I struggled to restrain myself from doing anything that might send me to a psychosis. Even though I was wide awake, my body was exhausted, and I could not reconcile reality and illusion. That evening, I left Tarragona Lodge and went to Hout Bay Hotel to check myself in, but I was told that the place was full. So, I called the Twelve Apostles Hotel to see if they had any availability. They said they did, and sent a driver to pick me up. When I got to the Twelve Apostles Hotel, I had a brief conversation with the front desk assistant and I told her that I would make a money-transfer to pay for my room but that never happened. It was late at night, but my energy was bursting at the seams. I ordered the biggest steak and a bottle of champagne. In between enjoying the food, I was dancing to the songs on tv, and doing a lot of 'planning' on my laptop. By this stage Katy Perry's 'Roar' was stuck in my head and the more I drank, the more I kept losing the plot.

According to Mood Disorders Society of Canada, *"...bipolar disorder is a medical condition which involves changes in brain function leading to dramatic mood swings."* While The Brain and Behavior Research Foundation (BBRF) describes bipolar disorder as *"...a brain and behavior disorder characterized by severe shifts in a person's mood and energy, making it difficult for the person to function."* However, the consensus is that bipolar disorder is a result of a chemical imbalance in a person's brain.

Without a doubt, the most effective way to alleviate the strain in the brain, is by taking medication prescribed by a doctor or psychiatrist. Bipolar disorder, or manic depression, as it used to be known, is primarily and most successfully treated with Lithium. Without medication: *"This mental disorder usually causes unusual shifts in your mood, energy, activity levels, concentration, and the ability to carry out day-to-day tasks,"* that is according to the BBRF. Other medications may include strong anti-psychotics to prevent psychosis.

67

What is psychosis? The National Institute of Mental Health (NIMH) calls it a *"...loss of contact with reality."*, where *"...a person's thoughts and perceptions are disturbed and the individual may have difficulty understanding what is real and what is not. Symptoms of psychosis include delusions (false beliefs) and hallucinations (seeing or hearing things that others do not see or hear). Other symptoms include incoherent or nonsense speech, and behavior that is inappropriate for the situation."*

Bipolar disorder is a big-tent disorder, and by that, I mean it covers a wide range of symptoms and behaviours. So, just to make things clear (or not), bipolar is split into two categories.

NIMH defines Bipolar Type 1 Disorder as *"Manic episodes that last 7 days, or by manic symptoms that are so severe that the person needs immediate hospital care."* This describes me when I was first diagnosed with bipolar disorder and ended up in hospital and again when I had another episode in my late 30s. Also, according to MIMH, Bipolar Type 2 Disorder is defined as *"...a pattern of depressive episodes and hypomanic episode, but not the full-blown manic episodes that are typical of Bipolar Type 1 Disorder."* Bipolar Type 2 Disorder is also a form of mental illness which is characterized by one's moods cycling between high and low. So, Bipolar Type 1 Disorder features the abnormal highs while Bipolar Type 2 Disorder is characterized by prolonged lows. However, the overwhelming difference between Bipolar Type 1 Disorder and Bipolar Type 2 Disorder, is that Bipolar Type

1 Disorder crosses over into psychosis. Psychosis is the defining feature of Bipolar Type 1 Disorder.

When I was diagnosed with Bipolar Type 1 Disorder, it meant that there was a gradual chemical progression in my brain which unfortunately was going to lead to psychosis. I rapidly went from being hypomanic and then without warning it escalated to full blown psychosis or mania. Therefore, I needed to be hospitalized and medicated before the mania escalated any further.

Good old Wikipedia defines "...*bipolar disorder 2 is a bipolar spectrum disorder characterized by at least one episode of hypomania and at least one episode of major depression. Diagnosis for Bipolar II Disorder requires that the individual must never have experienced a full manic episode. Otherwise, one manic episode meets the criteria for Bipolar Type 1 Disorder.*" Furthermore, NIMH says a "...*major depressive episode involves persisting depressed mood for at least two weeks. These periods may also involve an increase, decrease in appetite, or body weight, persisting insomnia or hypersomnia, persisting fatigue or energy loss, psychomotor agitation or slowing, feelings of worthlessness or excessive guilt, problems concentrating or making decisions and reoccurring thoughts of death or suicide.*"

Suicide is also a defining feature of bipolar. Statistically, "...*the rate of suicide among BD patients is approximately 10–30 times higher than the corresponding rate in the general population."*, according to 'Suicide Risk in Bipolar Disorder: A Brief Review' which can be found in the National Library of Medicine. These kinds of statistics are probably why my original psychiatrist called my bipolar 1 diagnosis a *terminal illness*. It doesn't have to be if you get the right diagnosis and treatment.

Hypomania can lead to mania, but the sad part at the time was that I did not understand what was happening to me. Healthline defines hypomania as *"...a milder form of mania." If you are experiencing hypomania, your energy level is higher than normal, but it's not as extreme as in mania. It causes problems in your life, but not to the extent that mania can. If you have hypomania, you won't need to be hospitalized."* To make matters worse, my hypomania progressed to mania very quickly. The severity of the symptoms and the intensity with which they increased was shocking.

Ultimately, there is a fine line between reality and psychosis and the disconnect from reality feeds into the psychosis which invariably translates to hallucinations, delusions and paranoia as the mania takes over.

When I was in my room at the 12 Apostles, I played music on the television and I danced the night away and then I decided to take a bath in order to relax and fall asleep, but I was still wide awake, with no possibility of sleep, in sight. I continued to listen to music, dancing along to songs by Beyonce and when I could not dance anymore, I would be on my laptop 'planning'. With my laptop in front of my face and the music playing in the background, I finally fell asleep around 3am. When I woke up around 8am to a knock on the door I was extremely disoriented, but soon I remembered where I was. I ignored the knocking.

I then got a call from the reception to say that I needed to settle the bill for the room. I took my time to go to the reception because it occurred to me that I did not have the money to pay for the hotel room. After promising to pay my bill, I went back to my room, but before that, I bumped into one of the staff members whom I remembered from my wedding. One minute we were chatting nicely and the next minute I started to shout at her, though I had no clue what this was about. I suspected that the drama was about the bill that needed to be paid. As the yelling escalated, Fin appeared out of nowhere and tried to defuse the situation, but I did not stop shouting. Eventually he took me to my room, it was locked so a staff member came to open the door for us, and we started packing up my things. Fin promised to pay for the room, and we drove back to Hout Bay.

Most of what happened after that is a bit vague, but I remember that Fin and I drove to Hout Bay. I also remember that Fin and I were shouting at each other and at some point, while he was driving, I tried to jump out of the moving car, but he pulled me back in the car and there was more shouting. When we arrived home, my mom and the kids were waiting for me. My mother was visibly heartbroken to see me in this state, but unfortunately this was just the beginning. I found it difficult to make sense of everything and as things in my mind got worse, it did not help that I was stuck in my own world. I remember a point where I was on social media thrashing various people and businesses. I escaped our home and for the next couple of days, I really lost the plot, the mania had fully taken over and I was hotel hopping between Mount Nelson hotel, the Table Bay hotel, and the Cullinan hotel. I spent the next few days going on little or no sleep and sadly this was taking a toll on my body and there was little I could do. Somewhere at the back of my mind I was aware that everything had gone pear-shaped, but unfortunately, I did not know what to do to stop the snowball effect. The crazy thing about mania (literally!), is at some point it feels like you are having an out of body experience and somehow, you know your brain is playing tricks on you. Everything is so distorted during mania, there is also a disconnect between reality and what your brain is telling you. Personally, my mania was such that it was controlling me, and it seemed like it was taking forever. I was not sure if I was coming or going. When the mania kicked in, I could not differentiate between what was real and what was not real. I was aggressive, paranoid and getting confrontational with people, especially with Fin and my mother.

After a whirlwind of moving around, a frantic Fin finally located me at the V&A Waterfront and he took me to the mall's information center where we could chat. I had an interview with one of the staff who asked me to tell him what was going on, and

Fin joined the interview. Two security guards drove me to Somerset Hospital, though my paranoid mind thought they were taking me to the airport so I could escape Cape Town. Fin met us there and took me in, where I was quickly diagnosed and then admitted to the psychiatric ward. I was still talking non-stop and mostly I was talking gibberish to the point that it seemed like I was struggling to catch my breath between words. In the psychiatric ward it was surprising to see so many people in one place. Before Fin went home, we had a chance to sit outside the courtyard and talk, but this was a struggle. When he spoke to me, I would revert to speaking gibberish. Back at the ward, I refused to take the medication the nurses gave me. Later I learned that if I refused to take my medication, I could easily be transferred to the 'notorious' Valkenburg Hospital for a minimum period of 6 months. When Fin came to visit me the next day, he begged me to take the medication. It was bad enough that I was going to miss Christmas with my boys, how much worse would it be if I were to be transferred to Valkenberg Hospital? So, I took the medication and I have not stopped taking my medication since.

I can never thank Fin and my mom enough for being kind and gentle when I was going through one of the most traumatic periods in my life. I cannot imagine what was going through my mom's head, when we were talking on the phone, I could hear the pain and exhaustion in her voice and that made me sad. She was pleased to hear that I was being discharged. It felt good to leave the hospital, as Fin picked me up and we went back home.

73

I could not help but admire how amazing and supportive Fin was through the entire process. When I got home, I was so thrilled to see the boys, I could not stop myself from hugging them. Aidan was chatting non-stop from excitement, and it was clear that Hope was so happy to see me back home. I was even more excited that Fin cooked dinner for us after the horrible food we had to eat at the hospital.

What I realized upon being back at home, is that it is not easy to bounce back from a psychotic breakdown like the one I had, but if you have a supportive environment and people that love you and you are willing to understand your illness- that, is half the battle. I had flashbacks from my mania which were rampant and as a result I would have to calm myself to deal with my anxiety. Initially I went for sessions with my psychiatrist, Dr Rausch, who had treated me for post-partum, but it turned out we were a bit mismatched. We were not agreeing completely on a lot of things, especially when it came to issues of religion or the lack thereof. This led me to seek out another psychiatrist.

My psychologist referred me to another psychiatrist, Dr. Tomcheck. She was so pleasant to work with and we hit it off immediately. The drive from Hout Bay to Oranjezicht was such a breeze especially since the drive passed by Table Mountain, and I would look forward to our sessions. I learnt something new about my illness every time I went. I also got the opportunity of understanding my medications and how they would help me.

Importantly, I did my own research on bipolar disorder and what treatment is available, and even explored acupuncture.

When you have any form of mental illness it is extremely important to take care of yourself. Be proactive about your medication because just by sticking to your medication you can circumvent a manic episode. Without a doubt, my medication is like the holy grail when it comes to treating my bipolar. If you are bipolar, please trust me on this issue, it could save your life.

It took a while for me to be diagnosed, and by the time I had my first mania, I had no clue as to how to proceed. Fortunately, I had the help and support of both my psychologist and psychiatrist. Still, I worried about having another episode and have since realized that there are 'signs' which might indicate that I am potentially hypomanic. It is a harsh reality to suddenly find yourself having to deal with a psychotic breakdown, when in fact the signs were so obvious in hindsight. When it's happening to you, it isn't always obvious what those signs are. Having a support network of family and friends you can trust, is one way to help identify the signs. Listen to them. Trust them. Let them help you help yourself.

Although it may be difficult to assist someone with hypomania, or someone who is in psychosis, that should not be a deterrent for giving them support. My gratitude goes to Fin because he has been my pillar of strength, not forgetting how my mom and my boys support me as well.

I have come a long way since I was first diagnosed with Bipolar Type 1 Disorder in Cape Town. But the danger of mania is always there, and I have since had another manic episode. Surviving bipolar has meant that, a lot about my life has changed drastically, and although there are still struggles, there are a lot of positive changes as well. Since being diagnosed, I have been following a strict regimen of medication -which I take religiously- followed by an exercise routine (I prefer road running). As much as I have learned that there is no 'one size fit all' when it comes to treating and caring for bipolar disorder, there have been many milestones in my journey, which remind me of the progress I make daily.

CHAPTER 6

Canada, my Home

"We must open the doors and we must see to it they remain open, so that others can pass through." ~ **Rosemary Brown**

Stability and routine are important tools for keeping bipolar under control.

Not long after my first mania, we made two important decisions; we decided to try for another child, and we decided it was time to raise our kids somewhere safer than South Africa. Both decisions made it exceedingly difficult to achieve stability and routine in my life, but I don't regret either one.

Things were so unstable that in the space of one year, we moved from Hout Bay to Olbia, Italy, back to East London in South Africa, and then to Canada. We have moved around a lot these past five years here in Canada, but things started to stabilize. We moved from Alton to Orangeville, from Orangeville to Amherstview, and now we are here in Kingston Ontario. I am full of excitement whenever we move to a new place, however I'm also aware of the stress it causes on my bipolar disorder. These relocations have also proven to be a revelation to me about my resilience, but the journey has been exhausting to say the least. I have been able to cope in all these new environments because of my medication, which helps me navigate my triggers. It also helps me function better day-to-day. All this moving has made it difficult to create support networks, whether it be professional, -like having a regular psychiatrist - or social, by having close friends I can rely on to give me feedback about my mental state. Most importantly, all this moving means I need to continuously pay attention to my mental health if I want to avoid another mania.

Let me begin with Italy. Sardinia is beautiful. We decided to relocate there because of the climate, the romance of living in Italy and because Fin had a job lined up. I remember stepping off the plane and instantly being engulfed by the sauna-like heat, to the point that I had a nosebleed. The locals were adamant that they had not seen that kind of weather since 1992. The heat was unbearable. It would often rise to more than 40 degrees Celsius. Our newborn, Connor, was only 4 months old when we moved to Sardinia, and he struggled with the heatwave as much as I did. We sought relief at the beach. The beaches in Sardinia are magnificent but getting there by bus with three boys was a mission. It's not that I couldn't acclimatize, as much as I didn't know how to. The fact that I spoke no Italian didn't help. Even though Fin had a job, things felt so temporary. We stayed in our apartment most of the day to be in the air-conditioning, only coming out in the evening for a stroll and maybe a meal.

I will say, that the food in Italy is insanely good.

Within two weeks of arriving in Sardinia, I knew that I did not want to be there. It was just too much, especially with Fin at work all the time. I had no support network to draw on and only social media and the kids to keep me company. It did not occur to me that I may have been suffering from post-partum depression at the time. I was very depressed, so it was entirely possible. Regardless, I became convinced that it would be better if we went back to South Africa. So, after two months of braving the heat, we decided that Fin would remain in Sardinia for a little while, thereafter he would investigate other sailing opportunities in Palma, Spain and then he too would come back to South Africa when there was some money in the bank.

At the end of August, I left with the boys on what would be a 28-hour journey with the end destination being East London. The boys and I said goodbye to Fin and flew from Sardinia to Rome; from Rome we flew to Qatar, from Qatar we flew to Johannesburg and finally from Johannesburg we flew to East London. By the time we arrived in East London I was exhausted and so were the boys, but we were thrilled to see my mom waiting for us at the airport. It was a serious challenge to fly with the boys, but with the help of the kind flight attendants I managed well between the flights.

In East London, I arranged a new school for Hope, nursery school for Aidan and baby Connor was going to stay at home with me. Fin was due to come back from Palma in November and this meant that we would have an opportunity to regroup and decide about how we were going to execute our new plan of immigrating to Canada. When Fin came back from Europe, we got our ducks in row and we agreed that we would start our journey over again. We stayed with my mom for 8 months but at the back of our minds, we were ready to move to Canada.

In May of 2016, just before Africa Day, we left South Africa for Canada. This was yet another journey which proved to be long and stressful, but at least Fin was there to give me a hand with the boys. We flew from East London to Johannesburg, Johannesburg to Heathrow, and from Heathrow to Toronto. We had a challenging 8-hour layover at Heathrow Airport- the boys were restless, hungry, and bored. We arrived in Toronto Pearson Airport on May 24, and we were picked up by my sister in-law Kate. We headed north of Toronto with our destination being Alton, where we would stay for a couple of months. The weather was warm and humid, but it was good enough for us because we had just come from a South African winter. We arrived at Kate's house, and we were welcomed by Kate's husband, Mike, and her daughter Suzanna-Rose. There was a lot of excitement because we had not seen each other for a while. We were going to stay at Kate's house for a couple of weeks and thereafter we would spend a month at Fin's dad's farm and then go back to Kate's house, until we found our own place. In October we eventually found a place of our own to rent in Orangeville and it was very cozy and centrally located. We really enjoyed our new home, and the boys especially enjoyed having their own space.

As lovely as our new home was, I still struggled with depression. I drank a lot of alcohol just to numb the pain of missing home. On one hand, I was excited because we were finally in Canada and living a fruitful life, and on the other hand, I was emotional, tired, irritable, and moody all the time. I had all the support I needed, especially from Fin and Kate, but it still was not enough to fill the void. I saw a doctor in Orangeville, who told me - after doing my bloodwork - that my Lithium levels were low. This meant that he had to increase my dosage of Lithium Carbonate from 300mg to 600mg. The doctor I saw was not a psychiatrist, but a General Practitioner (GP) and in Canada its normal for GPs to treat and prescribe medication for mental illness. After the doctor had increased my medication, I started to notice that I was getting better, and my moods were more manageable, and I was drinking less.

While we were getting used to our life in Canada, Fin and I started talking about the possibility of moving to Kingston Ontario. This made sense because Kingston has an impressive boating culture, and Fin was in the process of opening a sailing school. On July 1st we left Orangeville in two cars, and I could not believe how nervous I was to be driving in traffic on such a major highway. Luckily, all I had to do was to follow Fin who had our life packed into the back of a bakkie (truck). The highway had the worse bumper-to-bumper traffic I had ever seen- and that's saying something for someone who has lived in Johannesburg! According to Fin it was Canada Day, and everyone was travelling for the long weekend- just like Easter in South Africa. We settled in Amherstview, which is one of Kingston's surrounding suburbs- nervous about this new phase in our lives- but excited all the same.

Within a few weeks Fin was teaching sailing and was working hard at establishing his sailing school. The boys and I would occasionally take the 20-minute drive to Downtown Kingston to explore our new city. Other times we would take the Wolfe Island Ferry to enjoy a different scene just a twenty-minute boat ride from Kingston. The first time the boys and I went in the ferry, we were thrilled. We did not sit in the car, instead we went on the top level, and I took some amazing pictures. The Ferry ride from Kingston to Wolfe Island is twenty-minutes but it usually feels much shorter because there's so much to see. We had never been on a ferry before, so this was all so fascinating for us, especially the cars that were so neatly parked, allowing you to just leave your car and wonder around the boat. Other times we would get on the Kingston Trolly to explore Canada's first capital city on a 1-hour guided tour. The route is focused on the historic old town and downtown shopping district. In Kingston I felt it easier to acclimatize!

After the summer, I had to get the boys ready for the new school year which begins in the first week of September. The boys were incredibly nervous about their new schools, and they worried about whether the school would be a good fit or not. Fin and I assured them that things would be fine, and that they would make new friends, which was bound to be exciting. After a while, the boys settled, Hope was in high school, Aidan was in Senior Kindergarten and Connor was at day care twice a week. On the two days that Connor was at daycare, I got the house organized and I had time to catch up with all the necessary administration associated with running a household. I missed the boys a lot when they were at school because they kept me occupied, but at the same time I was relieved to have some time for myself.

Ironically, when I found myself with this free time, I used to feel a deep sense of loneliness and loss, and not even the texts and calls to and from South Africa could ease my longing for home. Like so many people who find themselves in foreign countries, the level of anxiety which comes with living in your new country is mind blowing - not to mention the uncertainty that comes with it. This is not a good space to be in if you are bipolar. I told myself I had to learn to be patient, to trust the process, take my medication, and take things one day at a time- but that is all easier said than done. It took a while to appreciate my own company. Not having any close friends around didn't help and making friends seemed like such an uphill battle. So, by October I started to pay more attention to my mood swings, and it occurred to me that I was not in a good space. I was very emotional and could not stop the bouts of depression I was experiencing, which came with anxiety and non-stop crying spells. It was time to see a psychotherapist.

The slow increase in my alcohol consumption, did not help the situation. The sessions occurred in the evenings and even though alcohol is a depressant, I treated it as an antidepressant, which proved to be disastrous. As soon as I put the kids to bed, I would continue with the drinking which had started when we were having dinner, and it would escalate into a serious drinking spree that would finish anytime between 1am and 3am. By this time, I would have been on the phone with anyone who cared enough to pick up when I was calling. More often than not, when I had to get the boys ready for school in the mornings, I would be so tired, drained, and dehydrated, that I struggled to fulfill my duties as a mom. Every morning I wished I could get rid of the hangover that was pummeling my head. It is astonishing how our bodies can take a pounding like that. For me, the signs that I was overdoing the drinking went unacknowledged. By the beginning of the evening, when I had recovered from the hangover I would be back to drinking until the early hours of the morning again. It was a vicious cycle and, typical of people who drink too much, I would get defensive when Fin mentioned my excessive drinking as a matter of concern. My drinking created so much tension between Fin and I, especially when Fin would discover that I slowly but surely had cleaned out our liquor cabinet. All this conflict was entirely due to the state of denial that I was stuck in. There was no doubt about it, I was now a habitual drinker, and it was not difficult for me to see that I was using alcohol to numb the pain of missing home.

Real pressure began in January of 2018 when Fin got an opportunity to work in the Caribbean- in St. Vincent and the Grenadines -for five weeks. This meant that I would be left at home with the boys. This proved to be a tremendous challenge because I was so used to parenting with Fin. I was suddenly going to be all alone, and though I did feel that I could do it, I also knew that I had no choice.

Soon after Fin left, my youngest son Connor got sick. His temperature was so high, and all I could do was give him Tylenol which is good for reducing a fever. I would also give him a cool sponge bath. This seemed to work for a while, but he would wake up again in the early hours of the morning, drenched in sweat and having cold shivers. I would repeat the same routine two or three times. I eventually took Connor to the Doctor, who said that he had a viral infection. This meant that all we could do, was let it run its course and I could use Tylenol whenever the need arose. As soon as Connor got better, Aidan got sick as well, having similar symptoms to his younger brother. Upon taking Aidan to the doctor, the doctor found a heart murmur, which terrified me. The doctor referred Aidan to a heart specialist to determine what kind of murmur it is. Aidan had an ultrasound done on his heart and it turned out to be an innocent heart murmur. According to the nurse who did the ultrasound, this kind of murmur can come and go throughout childhood. I have found, that being patient with myself and learning not to stress, is of vital importance during these experiences, because I was having to cope without the support from family and friends. When Fin came back, I had a real sense of accomplishment.

Being a mother comes with its own challenges, but after a while you get used to your role and familiarize yourself with the demands that come with it. I am glad to have reached a point where I can trust my own judgement when it comes to my kids. I am also fortunate to be raising my boys with a partner who is hands-on. I am grateful to have a partner who challenges me and prioritizes my happiness. Fin and I want only the best for our boys, which is why we came to Canada, and we will do whatever it takes to support them and ensure that they reach their potential. Most importantly, despite my homesickness, Canada has become home for us. Even with the chilly winters, we are grateful to be where we are.

We have moved a lot over the past few years, and each move has presented us with various challenges – some presenting us with more problems than solutions!

In an ideal world we would stay in one spot, and I would have the stability and daily routine I need, to keep anxiety and uncertainty from undermining my disorder. But real life just isn't like that, and Fin and I have had to weigh up the costs and benefits of each move- especially the way it affects my health. Moving to Canada has been a way to give our kids the stability *they* need. This is a country with a good education system, free health care and an abundance of wealth. It is also safe in a way that South Africa, sadly, is not. None of this would have been possible if I hadn't managed my bipolar. Moving to Canada was one of the best moves we've ever made. After 6 years of being here, we are content with our decision, even though I have since had to endure another mania and a big shake-up in our marriage.

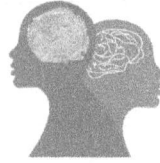

CHAPTER 7

The Seven Year Itch

"When it's gone, you'll know what a gift love was. You'll suffer like this. So go back and fight to keep it." ~ **Ian McEwan**

In the discussions we had about getting married versus not getting married, Fin made it clear he did not want to get married again. We had both been through divorces and the experience put Fin off the idea of marriage. On the other hand, I wanted to get married. Fin lost the argument and I started making plans for our wedding, which started with things such as looking at different wedding venues, cakes, flowers, and dresses. Fin was reluctant to take part in the wedding planning and because I understood where he was coming from, I let him be. After all it was 'my' wedding!

Back then I did not have any insight into the challenging work that goes into marriage. My first marriage had been very spontaneous and very brief. I did not have a good reference point for marriage because my mom's marriage and that of her two sisters ended in divorce.

Marriage is a very delicate thing and like an indoor plant it needs a lot of 'watering' and care. I think people can get confused over the difference between a wedding and a marriage. A wedding, is obviously the day that two people who are in in love come together in front of their family and friends, and promise to love and cherish one another in sickness and in health, for better or worse, till death do them part. A marriage on the other hand is different and complex. It is nuanced and layered in numerous ways that makes sense to the people involved. The uncomfortable truth about marriages, is that they are intricate and require a lot of patience to make them work. A marriage is not an event, it's a way of life.

Fin and I have been married for 10 years, but by the time of our seven-year anniversary- in 2018- came along, we were not doing well. Issues were piling up and our disagreements had become angrier and louder. I cannot say for certain how much of it is related to my bipolar and how much of it is just about being married, but I was easily offended and hurt whenever I felt Fin was being critical of me. I also didn't feel like he had my back. My relationship with his family was not going well and I felt like he was always taking their side over mine.

At the time, I was oblivious as to how many disputes I was getting into with people close to me. My mom visited that summer and things were great, until shortly before she left. I felt she was also taking sides against me. The subject of my rape came up and I was angry and felt she should accept some responsibility for what had happened. By the time she left, there was tension between us. I had not come to terms with my trauma, and it was becoming an issue in my life. No doubt it was also triggering my bipolar.

I felt very much that the people closest to me were not validating my feelings. I also didn't like that they were blaming my mood swings on being bipolar. By this time, I had a substantial number of 'friends' on social media and I sought validation from them. The more they supported me online the more I rejected my support network. Anyone who crossed me or questioned me on social media I got rid off with a click, 'ain't got no time for that'. If only real life was that simple, or maybe it was.

The arguments between Fin and I started small, but they grew in intensity. We fought a lot, and it didn't matter what the conflict was about, it just seemed to escalate, and it was a struggle to reconcile our differences. We soldiered on for a couple of months, but I was convinced our marriage was in trouble.

I would instantly become defensive whenever we talked about anything. Often, by the end of an argument, neither of us would have a clue as to why we were in a battle to begin with. At other times some of our arguments would take place in full view of our children, which was a deal-breaker for me. This was the one thing that I wasn't willing to tolerate in my marriage. Thankfully we never came to blows. I may have felt that Fin was being emotionally abusive, but he was never physically abusive.

Our relationship was not getting better so I decided to seek the services of a divorce lawyer because I lost any hope that my marriage could be salvaged. I felt that my emotions about the whole matter were justified. I no longer wished to be in a 'toxic' marriage.

On the last week of January 2019, I packed my bags and the boys' bags, and we left our home and went into a shelter for women. I had no job and nowhere else to go. Fin was not at home when we left, but upon his return from the boat show in Toronto, he must have realized that we were gone and called the Police. They told him that the boys and I were safe, but that he was not allowed to know where we were. I thought about how Fin would feel, and I imagined he was livid by what I had done, but I didn't care. Soon after that the boys and I were transferred from the Napanee women's shelter to another women's shelter in Kingston.

Fin found a lawyer who helped him gain access to the boys. When they were with their dad, I worried a lot, but I also knew how much Fin loved the boys and that made me feel a lot better. I found it challenging having to fight with Fin on the phone all the time. I blocked his number on many occasions when I felt things were too much. The amount of legal paperwork that was flying around was incredible and I was lucky that my lawyer was working pro bono. Fin was not so lucky. Eventually the lawyers worked out a 'custody agreement' which meant Fin had the boys one week and I had them the next until the courts reached a final decision on custody.

In Ontario, where we live, it takes a whole year before a couple can be granted divorce. This period is either designed to give the couple time to work on their issues or call it quits. Week-on week-off custody was strenuous. The boys were still attending the same school which meant that when they were with me, I would have to travel about 20 minutes to drop them off and pick them up. The whole separation was not only taking a toll on Fin and myself but on the boys as well. I can't imagine how the boys were taking it, but they seemed content to me and I felt awful for putting them through all this though. I would often reflect on how I felt when my mom divorced my dad and the impact this had on me.

In July I moved out of the shelter and into my own apartment, and I was so pleased to have my independence. I got a lot of support from various organizations especially those that deal with women who are displaced through abusive marriages. I had access to social welfare and was looking into finding work. When I was in the shelter, I tried my utmost best to keep working on myself and the question that came to mind, was "who am I and what exactly do I want out of life?" Having my own space was one of those answers.

When the boys were with me, I would make sure that we did a lot of activities, and I relished every moment of spending time with them. On occasion, I would talk with them about the separation, but I could tell it was not something they particularly wanted to talk about. Meanwhile, Fin and I were still in conflict which meant that communication between us was done via the lawyers, and we could not see eye to eye on anything- especially on issues related to the boys' upbringing. It proved to be a mission to try to have a good relationship with Fin and the level of animosity between us was astonishing.

Although things seemed tough for both of us on a personal level, the legal stuff was a train wreck. At times we had to appear in court as our case progressed and I would resent having to be there at all. There were so many emails to be read, damaging text messages that were sent and not to mention the calls that were fueled by anger and resentment. I was so angry that I decided at one point that I wanted full-custody and legal negotiations collapsed. A social worker tried to mediate but I rejected his conclusions. The more my lawyer recommended settling the more I wanted to fight.

I hate to think about how confused the boys were about what was going on. This confusion- which also included the back and forth between the two houses- worried me, as I did not know the impact the divorce was having on them. Would it stunt their emotional growth? Would it lead to years of undealt with trauma? I would watch the boys like a hawk, and constantly be on the lookout for any changes in their behaviour. I found it challenging to sit the boys down and talk to them about the divorce and the separation. Apart from Hope - who was older- the kids couldn't fully understand much of what was going on. It's not easy worrying that your children may be falling through the cracks due to divorce- no matter how you try to protect them.

I thought I was doing a good job of taking care of myself. I was still taking my medication, I was going to therapy, and I did a lot of road-running. On a good day I would run an equivalent of a half-marathon. However, with all the running I was doing, and the amount of water I was consuming, I didn't realize that I was at risk of diluting the lithium in my system. This was dangerous because the lithium was being used to treat my mania. I felt dehydrated most of the time and the more water I drank, the less impact the lithium would have. I was in great shape, but I simply could not stop the crying spells. I lost a lot of weight, and my appetite was so irregular that I did not know whether I was coming or going.

Apart from all the running I was doing, and the therapy sessions, I honestly have no idea how I coped. The entire year was full of never-ending drama - conflict, lawyers, arguments, and court appearances were the norm. I was in denial of the fact that I was probably in an advanced state of hypomania. Also, it didn't occur to me that I could be having trouble related to my medication, I just took the pills out of habit and without thinking that there might be anything weird going on. Even though I was religiously taking my medication, it never struck me that I was doing more harm than good just from a simple thing like drinking lots of water.

By September of 2019, I started feeling overwhelmed, despondent, and anxious about everything. I couldn't tell where all of it was coming from. I just felt this enormous strain on my shoulders. I would feel so drained, especially when it was time to focus on the legal stuff. My emotions were intense and at times they were upside down. I remember how excited I was when it was my week to have the boys, but that excitement would be short-lived and replaced by anxiety. I felt as though I had something to prove to them and myself. I like to think I still managed to be the mother they could count on, even during all the drama that was unfolding and despite my surging hypomania.

Other times I would have high energy levels and feel very positive about myself and how I looked. I've always enjoyed posting pics on social media but now I was craving the likes and comments I got when I strutted my stuff online. But there was a lot of poor decision-making - especially with money - which was a result of my increasing impulsivity. Then suddenly, I was a social-media wrecking-ball, having a lot of arguments with different people- resulting in a lot of broken relationships. Most of the time I saw myself as the victim - okay, I *always* saw myself as the victim. I was also sending some very explosive emails, and in those emails, one could tell that I was not only abrasive but unstable as well.

I often think to myself, how hard marriage is, and how it becomes even harder when compounded by complex things such as mental illness. It's easy to say, that the key is to ensure that you have healthy communication lines with your partner and that you should both strive for mental wellness- but it's just not that easy. I thought we were doing those things, but it all unraveled in a short space of time in late 2018. My bipolar disorder made it impossible to deal with it normally. The following year was not only the worse year of my life, but it also shook me to the core. As the summer of 2019 ended it was becoming more and more apparent to everyone except me that I was heading for another breakdown.

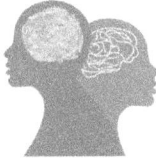

CHAPTER 8

Organized Chaos

"All great changes are preceded by chaos." ~ **Deepak Chopra**

When you are dealing with mania, it becomes exceedingly difficult to comprehend the extent of the mania yourself. You are stuck somewhere between reality and delusion. That's precisely what was happening to me in late October and early November of 2019. It culminated in this moment I remember, when I could somehow feel that my mania was taking off and I could do nothing to control it.

Fin came over to my apartment to drop off the boys for my custody week and we had an argument about something - I cannot even remember what it was about- and I slammed the front door on him. As he was leaving, he angrily kicked the bottom of the door, probably in frustration in having to deal with me. As a result, my paranoia kicked in and I suddenly became terrified of what Fin might do to me. The kick of the door, which wasn't anything, turned into a super big deal in my mind and I became convinced Fin wanted to hurt me. I decided we had to leave Kingston immediately. We had to run. I started randomly packing most of my stuff and the boy's stuff as well, into suitcases, boxes, and garbage bags. It must have taken a good 3 to 4 hours to get it done. For some time, I had no idea why I was packing anymore, I was just packing. I turned my apartment upside down because the packing went from just being about clothes to packing weird household items like knick-knacks, trinkets, and the odd kitchen utensil as well. The car was filled to the brim, and I had no idea where the boys would fit.

I remember that amid all the packing, a friend of mine, Marilyn, came over to give me some money, just in case I ran into a situation where I might need cash (I had spent all my money impulsively over the previous weeks). I can only imagine what I told her. Sometime in the middle of the night me and my boys were on the road to Ottawa. Time seemed to be moving quite fast, and the 2-hour drive from Kingston to Ottawa felt more like a flash. I was not paying attention to the speed limit, as I was in such a hurry. When we arrived in Ottawa, I used my phone's navigation system to locate the South African Consulate. At this point it was not clear to me, why I wanted to go to the Consulate, I just had to get there. The first thing I did when we arrived at the Consulate, was to bend the license plates up to conceal them. I was extremely paranoid, and I guess I was worried about being tracked by Fin. The younger boys were sleeping amongst our things in the backseat while Hope sat next to me in the front passenger seat, wide awake. Even in my compromised state of mind I could see he was worried.

The South African Consulate is located at 25 Sussex Drive, which is a prestigious address in Ottawa. 22 Sussex Drive, which is across the road, is the home of the Canadian Prime Minister, and, at the time, I had no idea. I was still wondering what to do next when suddenly the whole area was flooded by the Royal Canadian Mounted Police (RCMP) and the Ottawa Police. The RCMP asked me a lot of questions about why I was at the Consulate at 2am, they also wanted to know why I bent the license plates the way I did. They were puzzled by the fact that I drove from Kingston to Ottawa after midnight, with young children. However, I could not give them a straight answer because I also had no clue what I was doing there. I was seriously struggling to articulate the reason I was at the Consulate. I was talking non-stop and making absolutely no sense. Using their database, the RCMP picked up who the owner of the car was, and then they called Fin. There was a lot of confusion over my intentions. Hope helped by explaining we weren't a threat but once they spoke to Fin, they got the background of our story. I could not gauge what Fin said to the Ottawa Police, but I know that he alerted them to my bipolar disorder. There were more calls made and one of those calls was to Children's Aid to come for the boys. I was being taken into custody.

Everything was happening so fast and because of my mania, I could not keep up with what was happening. The sad part is that I was constantly trying to remember things but the fight in my brain between sanity and insanity was escalating. At some point the police were trying to decide what to do with me and believe it or not the RCMP wanted to detain me under Canada's Anti-terrorism Act. It was Fin's conversation with an Ottawa Police sergeant that eventually tipped the scales.

Thankfully when all of this was happening, the younger boys were sleeping in the backseat, so I don't think they got to hear or witness all the drama which had been unfolding around them. Hope, however, was still sitting in the front passenger seat and one of the police officers asked him to step out of the car, so that they could have a chat. One of the questions Hope was asked was "does your mom normally behave the way she is behaving now" to which Hope responded with a "yes?". Not helpful.

After some more impossible questions from the police, I was asked to get out of the car, and they told me that two officers were going to take me to the nearby hospital where a psychological assessment would be done. The final decision would rest with the doctors who would attend to my case. The only person who could have told the police about my mental health status was Fin and at that moment I resented him so much for 'broadcasting' my illness.

Before they took me to the hospital, they put handcuffs on my wrists. I was taken to hospital while my children remained with them. I had no idea of what would happen to the boys. I was sad to think that I put my boys through all that and I felt even worse when I thought about what would happen to them in my absence. I had no idea that my mania had endangered my children. I had no choice but to leave the boys with police, with the hope that they would be taken back to their father.

If you ever take the time to think about how people with mental illness are treated, just look back in my story to the way my aunt was treated by the men who were chasing her and then look at the fact that I was put in handcuffs before I was taken to the hospital. We are treated as a danger to others - which is how society views people who suffer from mental illness - and we are restrained. No paramedics assessed me, I wasn't tranquilized, there was no emergency psychotherapist trying to reach out to what little sanity was left in my mind. Just burly police officers with guns and tasers and very little ability to judge mental health situations. I'm glad this happened in Canada, as in America I could have been shot. It's seriously time that we rethink how we deal with circumstances which may involve mental illness. There must be a better, more humane way to handle these events. Yes, they have a hard job but at the very least we must start with the police.

After I was put in handcuffs, one of the two police officers helped me get into the police car and we left for the nearest hospital. I was incredibly surprised when he thanked me for not trying to run away just before they handcuffed me. Would they have shot me if I had? It's Canada, so I hope not. It was a short drive to the hospital, but for me it seemed longer. As I watched streetlamps disappear behind me, I wished that I could disappear and not have to deal with all the drama of the night. I was taken to the Royal Ottawa Hospital, and I had to wait for a while before being seen by the attending psychiatrist. I was so manic that it was challenging to be fully present. My thought processing was incomprehensible, and I was struggling to make a distinction between reality and fiction.

The interview I had with the psychiatrist and her colleague was not the best- I was abrasive, aggressive and downright rude to them. It felt like my cognitive abilities were failing me, and the more they failed me the more annoyed I became. After the initial interview, I was transferred to the psychiatric ward where a nurse did an intake interview, and I was shown my room and given medication- which I had enough sense to take. I was so used to taking my medication, that by this point in my bipolar life I don't think I even contemplated not taking them. My first day at the hospital was very rough but at least the nurses were genuine and nice. I remember only a few details about being hospitalized but I kept thinking how pristine the hospital was, how friendly the staff were and just how the hospital looked more like a hotel than a hospital. The state of the psychiatric ward looked far more advanced, organized, and exceptionally clean compared to Sommerset hospital back in Cape Town.

The second day of being at the hospital, mostly involved me insisting on talking to someone at the South African Consulate. It was all very confusing, and I still had no notion of what I was doing there. I was given more medication to reduce the impact of the mania. A mood stabilizer and an anti-psychotic were prescribed, which I took. My lithium dosage was doubled from 600 milligrams to 1200 milligrams. The doctor said they would check back to see if I was making any progress. It was all very pleasant and professional.

After a couple of days, I got used to the routine and I was taking the medication without any problems. It was working. I found the group meetings appealing, particularly where we could do arts and crafts, and these became an outlet for me- especially where I couldn't express myself properly in words.

After more than a week, and when the doctors felt that my medication was doing its job, I was discharged. The psychiatric ward was full, and even in Canada the mental health system is strained to the point of breaking, so I was let go when it was felt I was reasonably stable.

On the day I was leaving, I took a cab to the train station, to take a train back to Kingston. The train ride was pleasant, it was the beginning of November, and it had snowed. It was so delightful to watch field upon field covered with snow and the sunset looked so bright. On the train, I kept thinking about everything which led to me being hospitalized and I realized just how dire the situation had been. I thought about the boys a lot on that train ride. I could not wait to see them and hug them and reassure them that mommy is 'fine'. When I arrived in Kingston, I took a cab back to my place and I called Hope who had been staying with a friend. When he arrived at my place, I was so happy to see him, but I wondered how he was coping in my absence. Not good as it turns out. I called my friend Lana to let her know I was back from the hospital. She stood by me through thick and thin and still does. I was dreading the fact that I had to call Fin to check on the boys, but I called him anyway and we talked about the schedule for the boys. I didn't realize it at the time, but my manic event almost certainly derailed any hope I had of having full-custody of the boys, and in fact it was highly likely that Fin would now have full-custody. Still, he never objected to them spending time with me.

Hope was staying with me at the time and because he was 16 years old, it was up to him to decide on who he wanted to live with. When Fin and I first split up he came with me to the woman's shelter, but soon found it too much of a strain and decided to live with Fin full time so he could attend his high school and be close to his friends. He also blamed me for the break-up, and we stopped talking to each other. With two parents at each other's throat, he decided to self-medicate with cannabis. Fin struggled to control him and eventually Hope was expelled from his high school. As the tension increased between the two of them Hope reached out to me. I was hypomanic and happy to indulge his new lifestyle choices, after all I was the 'cool' parent. But when I returned from the hospital, I could see things weren't going well for him.

It didn't take long for the animosity between Fin and I to subside. This meant that we were now able to be cordial towards each other. We were not in conflict, and it was a little easier to communicate without the baggage or drama brought on by being hypomanic. By the end of November, we started to become more comfortable with each other and we were both very conscious of the fact that it was time to reduce the tension. This is where we got the opportunity to start communicating positively and be considerate of each other's schedule. Fin and I decided to put aside our differences and put our children's needs first and avoid getting into arguments. It had already been a longtime of fighting and now it was time to heal and move on. This was very much dependent on how 'mature' we were going to be about our relationship. Whether it was something in me that clicked, or Fin saw me in a different light, or it was the medication that I was taking, something in me did 'click' and I realized I was still in love with Fin.

One night, when Fin had the boys, I decided to go to a jazz club where I enjoyed watching a live band and I was so happy to be surrounded by people, even though I did not know any of them. It was nice to chat with other people and feel normal again. After the jazz session, I went home and Hope was not there. He had gone to his friend's house, and he had my house keys and I ended up calling Fin. We had a civil conversation, but he was in bed and not impressed with me calling so late or the fact that I had time to go to a jazz club while he had to work and look after the boys. My reply to Fin was that he too could go and enjoy some jazz if he wanted to, and I offered to take the boys the next night, even though it was his turn to be with them. Instead of wanting to fight him I decided to reach out. Soon after that conversation Fin asked me to go for coffee with him, and I agreed. It turned out to be one of the best dates we have ever had. We talked about a lot of things including the possibility of getting back together, but we both agreed that we would have to take things slowly.

One of the things that helped me deal with Fin, was hearing that he was also in therapy. We both felt that any talk of getting back together would require couples counselling, so we began the process. It didn't happen overnight but it became apparent to both of us that we wanted to be together again. We had been through too much together to not give it a second chance, and I'm eternally grateful that we did. Where our boys are concerned, it has been delightful to see how happy they are and how much they adjusted to all the changes.

Logistically we now had two households. We decided not to move into our places but to find somewhere new that didn't have any bad memories. We have since moved into a new townhome which we both like and the boys are simply delighted to see mom and dad in the same house.

My bipolar is inconsistent and unpredictable, which means it is important to have a family or a network of people who care about me, and who I can trust. When I was struggling with my disorder prior to our separation, I used social media to frame my life with Fin as a burden. I painted a picture which my social media 'friends' were quick to accept and reflect back to me as being 'toxic'. I chose this narrative over trusting what the people who know me and love me were trying to tell me- they were telling me that there might be a problem with my bipolar.

It gets difficult sometimes to make sense of my reality and the illusions I have about myself, as I'm sure it does for everyone. However, being bipolar amplifies everything- the good and the bad. It affects how I react to things, especially when I'm hypomanic. It absolutely affected everything about my separation from Fin, and before I knew it, I was in psychosis once again.

Being hospitalized for mania or any other form of mental disorder is not designed to embarrass you in any way. While hospitalization can make you feel guilt and shame, it is best to think about it as getting the right treatment and care. I have been truly fortunate to have had the opportunity to re-connect with my family, and I have really appreciated all the support I have been getting from Fin and the boys. It has been quite a journey- one that makes me look back and wonder where I got the strength to fight all my demons. While I embrace all the positive changes in my life, I have also learned to discard all the things that no longer serve me well, and it is important to make a distinction between the two.

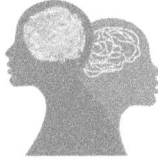

CHAPTER 9

Pursuit of Happiness

"Be fearless in the pursuit of what sets your soul on fire."
~ Jennifer Lee

Life in general, is a fickle thing, largely because of its unpredictable nature. You think you know what to expect, and yet it seems like the more you think you've got all of it figured out, the less you know. What's with all these absurd ups and downs? Life for me, has been nothing short of a roller coaster ride because of my bipolar- more so than it is for 'normal' people. I have a mood disorder, which amplifies these ups and downs, to a degree that is unmanageable without medication. I mean, who would be able to go through my worst bipolar experiences and not feel tainted by them? However, I don't allow that to stand in the way of living my life. Having to go through two manias in a space of 6 years, and still come back from them and achieve 'normal' functionality as a human being, is nothing short of victorious. This to me, is something special and character building. As strong as I am right now, I am humble enough to recognize just how far my family is willing to go to support me and how their unconditional love keeps me going.

What also drives me is this very human concept called 'pursuit of happiness'. It's human to want to be happy, isn't it? And I want to be happy. However, happiness can be very elusive for people with bipolar disorder, and I would like to talk about that, because I think bipolar people struggle to find happiness.

So, what comes to mind when we talk of the 'pursuit of happiness' as a concept? When we unpack the idea, we might think of things like, where does happiness begin, where does it end and how does it affect us? What does happiness look like? Is it smiling selfies on social media, or maybe something a bit deeper than that? If you walked a mile in my shoes, you would realize that my 'pursuit of happiness' has been this absurdly turbulent never-ending journey. It is hard to be happy and depressed at the same time. In my case, I often wonder if I am meant to ever reach the end of this great pursuit, and if I do, is it sustainable? I have recently started to think of the 'pursuit of happiness' as a state of mind. It is a journey in which you nurture and harness your moments of happiness, however brief, to give a positive meaning to your life.

In the American context, 'the pursuit of happiness' is defined as: *"…a fundamental right mentioned in the Declaration of Independence to freely pursue joy and live life in a way that makes you happy, as long as you don't do anything illegal or violate the rights of others."* I really like the above definition because its straight to the point and I also like the fact that it highlights happiness as something to be pursued without infringing on the rights of anyone else. Before I could even think about my own pursuit of happiness, I had to work through other emotions that I was struggling with. After both my manias, I did feel an enormous sense of shame and guilt, and this was simply because of the drama that came with each episode. I hurt people close to me, not physically, but with words and my behavior. It's hard to have any sense of confidence and self-esteem when you realize the amount of carnage you've been responsible for. But how do you apologize for behaviour you couldn't control?

We all know how discouraging it can be when your confidence or self-esteem takes a hammering, and a bipolar person can become afflicted with shame and guilt in large measures. According to mighty Wikipedia *"shame is an unpleasant self-conscious emotion typically associated with a negative evaluation of the self; withdrawal motivations; and feelings of distress, exposure, mistrust, powerlessness and worthlessness."* Guilt on the other hand is *"…a moral emotion that occurs when a person believes or realizes- accurately or not - that they have compromised their own standard of conduct or*

111

have violated universal moral standards and bear significant responsibility for the violation." I have felt both in the aftermath of a mania, and the effect is oppressive.

After being manic, I had to contend with bouts of depression, which at times felt like I was being choked. Usually, I would be extremely hard on myself- full of self-doubt and basically set off on a journey of self-sabotage. For instance, with the recovery from my mania I had to wait until my medication kicked in before I could even begin to contemplate happiness. In all this, I consoled myself by taking into account that everything takes time and that eventually, I would be better. The first time I went through a manic episode this was quite difficult, but the second time I was able to help myself- which is why going to therapy every week has been an important part of the recovery process. I also choose to surround myself with people who are patient, kind and have a positive mindset. This too can be difficult if you have hurt them in some way during the manic process. As resilient as I must be, so too do the people who care about me.

Happiness means different things to different people, obviously. It's a subjective experience which unfolds in various layers. For me, going down this path to happiness means reaping the benefits of what I put into this journey- I must put in the effort if I want to be happy. Oftentimes, for me, happiness ends up being the journey itself. It's the sifting through these layers which gives me a better understanding of where I am going and helps me decide where I want to be in life. After all, happiness is comparative. It's impossible to know what happiness is if you haven't experienced unhappiness, which bipolar disorder provides plenty of. I think the 'pursuit of happiness' is really a process of 'self-discovery', where the amount of energy we put into cultivating happiness matters. It matters a lot.

I often would think that if I find happiness, I can look forward to having some peace in my life and some relief from this unrelenting mood disorder we call bipolar. It's just not that easy. For instance, on my quest for happiness I have come to realize that bipolar disorder presents so many hurdles to jump over that stumbling over one of them feels like it can make or break my goal of being 'happy'. Mania recovery is a perfect example.

After experiencing a manic episode, everything seems like such an effort and apart from spending time with the boys, I was just not interested in anything else. I also struggled to piece my life together and it felt like my entire system was being rebooted and I was simply starting over. I told myself I must be open to re-inventing myself or nothing will happen. The responsibility for guarding my happiness becomes mine and mine alone. Sometimes you will have the feeling that you will never reach your happiness, or that it seems impossible to attain, but you must persevere and believe that you are worthy of happiness. When I look at my journey of living with bipolar disorder for 8 years, I know very well that my pursuit of happiness will not look the same as someone who is not diagnosed with bipolar. Therefore, I must take extra precautions to avoid triggers that can come from anywhere and potentially disturb my peace and happiness, or worse drive me into another manic episode. But I've learned to treat these hurdles as sacrifices I need to make to reach my 'destination'.

The thing about starting over is that you get a chance to, look at where you are versus where you come from. It's how you feel about where you are in life and most importantly you get to readjust your position according to what you think is best for you. In my case though, it felt like I was learning to do things for the first time, and I had to wait until I was post mania to take baby steps towards everything. As an example, before I had mania, I could easily open a book and read it without any issues. After I had my first mania, my attempt at reading anything was just dismal, and this left me despondent and demoralized. Reading a book was such a chore and an uphill battle. I struggled to read fast enough and trying to comprehend what I was reading was a challenge. The book I was reading at the time after my first mania was 'Sane New World' by Ruby Wax and though I struggled to read it, I could not put it down. It's a wonderful take on her own manic depression and her own struggles. I could relate to her. But it took forever.

Here is how I look at happiness at this point in my life. The pursuit of happiness for me is about making a conscious decision to look after my mental health, to take my medication and most importantly be surrounded by the people I love. It also means getting out of my comfort zone now and then and taking small risks which will potentially enhance my life – like writing this book. It begins with small steps -which may appear insignificant at the time- but that can add up to modest milestones which in turn add up to these tangible accomplishments which have a positive impact on my life journey. Writing this book was good for me. Simple things now bring me real happiness. It's so fulfilling being immersed in what my boys are doing, or simply playing games with them or finishing a 10km run.

This is another way of ensuring that I'm happy. I stay active, healthy and I have road running as my outlet. There is a real link between physical activity and mental wellness.

The pursuit of happiness for me also means accepting my bipolar disorder and the stages it takes me on. At times it means that I just ride the wave until it is over, whereas previously I fought against my mania which led to my manic state being worse. Happiness for me is also relying on the medication I take for bipolar. *Lithium Carbonate* is a mood-stabilizer and a life saver. According to WebMD *"Lithium as it is known, is one of the most widely used and studied medications for treating bipolar disorder"*. Furthermore, WebMD reveals that *"...studies show that Lithium can significantly reduce suicide risk and it can also prevent future mania and depressive episodes."* I know I've made the point earlier in this book, but I can't say enough about how well lithium works. I also take *Risperidone* because it is an antipsychotic pill designed to prevent psychosis. Lastly, I also take *Escitalopram* for depression. In the beginning of taking this medication, I was skeptical about how long it will take to kick-in, but with time I got used to them and they seemed to be working just fine. However, every three months my doctor checks my Lithium levels to establish how the Lithium is interacting with my whole body and how my thyroid, kidneys and liver are functioning. This is one of the few ways my doctor can determine how well the medication is working and if there are any side-effects that have occurred.

For me, thinking about pursuing happiness is now within the realm of my bipolar disorder. Engaging in things which enhance my mental health is paramount to my healing. As long as I'm sticking to my treatment, therapy and exercise then I know I have moved a step closer to my happiness. It seems like whenever I do something for my happiness, I must think about whether it makes sense for me or whether it's my bipolar influencing me or both.

Sometimes I wonder how things would have turned out had I not been diagnosed with bipolar disorder, but I soon realize that this exercise is a waste of my time. The 'pursuit of happiness' is something that resonates with me; the road to pursuing my happiness hasn't been easy but each day presents me with an opportunity to do things differently and somehow that gives me a lot of peace. I hope it does the same for you.

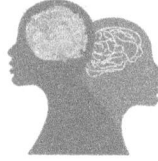

CHAPTER 10

On Top of the World

"You may encounter many defeats, but you must not be defeated. In fact, it may be necessary to encounter the defeats, so you can know who you are, what you can rise from, how you still come out of it." ~ **Maya Angelou**

I like this quote by Maya Angelou, because it encapsulates all the things which are untangling in my life. You never know how strong you are until you must be strong. It has been a long time coming but I finally have the confidence, to not only challenge my environment, but to also be in tune with my limitations. I feel like I finally have some insight into bipolar disorder.

The following guidelines are some steps which may help you and those close to you contend with mental illness. Hopefully they will help you understand and enhance the quality of your life as they have for me. Here goes:

1. EDUCATE YOURSELF & OTHERS: It used to be difficult to diagnose mental illness, which made it extremely difficult to prescribe medication essential to battling the illness. Those who were visibly suffering from mental illness could be misdiagnosed and/or neglected. Although strides have been made in improving and raising awareness, society in general looks down on people with mental illness and the discussions we are having about mental wellness are few and far between. In South Africa, if I think about the number of people with mental illness and look at how our townships treat people who are struggling mental illness and I am appalled. So, whether you are surviving mental illness or supporting someone who is afflicted by mental illness, it should be everyone's duty to educate themselves and learn more about mental health and offer support where you can.

2. GET PROFESSIONAL HELP: I was 15 years old when I first saw a psychologist and it felt strange to sit down with a man who I considered to be a stranger and talk with him about my issues, but the session was a revelation. It made me think deeper about issues related to mental health. Therapy is just one way to treat mental health. Seeing a psychiatrist is also important, and despite my current state of mind, I find it disheartening to realize that I was 33 years old before I finally saw a psychiatrist who gave me the right diagnosis. If I had understood my condition, I might have been more prepared. So, while it isn't always easy to find the 'right' help, it is important to seek out 'professional' help. It is necessary to seek medical intervention, simply because this allows the sufferer to deal with the effects of mental illness in a space where they feel heard and supported.

3. ADDRESS THE STIGMA: Everything that is difficult about dealing with mental health is compounded by the stigma attached to mental illness, especially when people think you are being 'punished' by God. Stigma can alienate a person who suffers from mental illness and keep them from seeking help. Although stigma can be both subtle and downright confrontational - whichever way it manifests- it is still stigma. According to the South African National Human Rights Plan, "stigma refers to negative beliefs, attitudes and feelings towards people based on characteristics seen as 'different' to those thought to be 'acceptable' characteristics of a person". Waiting for governments to educate the population on mental illness to help remove the stigma might take forever, so let this journey to destigmatize mental illness begin at home and with the family. Let it begin with you.

4. DO NOT DISCRIMINATE: Discrimination is "…linked to stigma and refers to behaviour or action towards people based on negative beliefs, attitudes, and feelings. It occurs when people act on their stigmatizing beliefs, attitudes and feelings in ways that are harmful to the stigmatized person and impacts on their rights"- according to South African National Human Rights Plan. Without doubt, Africans should understand the negative impacts of discrimination. People with mental illness are often unable to find work or are shunned by society. This is not right. If we want to address mental health issues in society then we need more empathy. We need to find ways to protect people with mental illness, not alienate them. More importantly, often you will find that people struggling due to mental illness will be reluctant to get help simply because they do not want to deal with discrimination. Reach out, don't discriminate. Ubuntu.

5. EMBRACE MEDICATION: There is nothing wrong with taking medication. People take medicine for HIV, heart disease and all sorts of things, and yet so many people with mental illness want to avoid the stigma associated with taking medication for mental health issues. If you are a person who suffers from depression or suspect that you suffer from suicidal thoughts, it is important to get help and be medicated. If you have been diagnosed with bipolar disorder or any other mental illness, it is best you that you stick to taking your medication, that you understand your medication and have a good relationship with your psychiatrist or doctor. It is also crucial that you take an active role in seeking the right medication by giving feedback to your doctors. This could save your life.

6. DEAL WITH TRAUMA & TRIGGERS: Trauma that has not been dealt with is like a ticking bomb and it is more dangerous to think that it will simply go away or not be an issue anymore as you get older. In my case for instance, I experienced sexual abuse as a child, and I grew up being an awkward child with a secret in my chest. I am fortunate to have all the love and support of my family. I am not sure how Black families deal with sexual abuse, but I can recall from conversations that I've had with various people, that when the 'secret' is discovered, there is usually a debate by the family as to whether this violation will be reported to the police or not. Unfortunately reporting the trauma also has its own set of complications. Addressing the trauma is the best way to come to terms with it. It may take time but until it is dealt with it will always be a trigger which can increase mental health episodes.

7. DON'T SELF-MEDICATE: In so many cases, when the effects of sexual abuse manifest itself in the form of mental illness, drinking and drugs seem to be the best medicine. They aren't. Nor is careless sexual behaviour, especially in South Africa with so much HIV. Alcohol acts as a depressant and drugs can mess-up the already messed-up chemistry in the mind of a mentally ill person. Ask your doctor if you want the opinion of a professional.

8. TRUST THE SUPPORT NETWORK: If you have people close to you, let them help you understand when you need help. Trust the fact that they have your best interests at heart. It may not seem like that, especially if paranoia is part of your disorder, but have faith in them. Don't let social media reinforce your delusions about yourself, listen to those close to you instead.

9. RESPECT YOURSELF, YOU ARE NOT ALONE: There are so many people affected by bipolar disorder and mental illness all over the world. There is nothing 'wrong' with you and you are not being punished for anything. Mental illness is about brain chemistry not supernatural mumbo jumbo. Respect yourself enough to seek out help.

10. LEARN TO BEND: Being bipolar is going to mean adjusting to the disorder, adjusting to medication, and reshaping your life. This can be an opportunity to gain experience and find happiness. It also means finding coping mechanisms which help you deal with day-to-day life as someone who is bipolar. Have a routine, meditate or get exercise, and find ways to be kind to yourself.

We live in an age where technological advances allow us to freely access information and other services and therefore, I think there's hope for the future particularly when it comes to mental health therapies, medication and most importantly how we talk about mental illnesses and mental health. Hopefully, the time between episodes and treatment shrinks so that people can get the help they need. I do hope that this book will encourage people to be open and honest about their struggles, so that we can have meaningful discussions about mental health. Everything that is highlighted in this book is aimed at giving insight into a phenomenon that affects both women and men who can relate to my story. It is also my hope that those women, especially African women, will be able to identify triggers which may potentially drag them back into the same darkness that they are trying to escape from.

It has been two and a half years since I had my second mania and currently my medication and yoga keep me balanced. Luckily, there are no signs indicating that I might go through another episode. I have learned a lot about myself, my coping mechanisms, my resilience, my courage. Through the process of falling ill and subsequently being diagnosed with Bipolar Type 1 Disorder, I have realized that my strength keeps me going. I am content with the fact that the various treatments and therapies associated with mental health have given me the opportunity to heal and cope as I live a full life. Mental illness is real, it is severe, and it affects ordinary people in diverse ways. Mental illness is not a farfetched or random illness that you pick up along the way, instead it should be taken seriously and treated with care.

The last 6 years have been quite a ride for me and my family but as we continue this journey, we feel content in knowing that we will be fine. We are doing everything in our power to ensure that the boys are doing well, and all their needs are met. I do want to say, that through some of my darkest times over the last ten years, I got to appreciate Fin for all the patience, love and support he has given me -especially when I was in the height of my mania. I want to thank my mother as well, for being open-minded and loving and never giving up on me.

At times I may feel overwhelmed by my mental health status, but I don't let it become too much for me anymore. All the love and support that I have received and continue to receive from my friends and family has meant so much to me and I would not trade it for the world. I can honestly say that I feel like I'm catching up to this strange thing we call 'sanity'.

www.ingramcontent.com/pod-product-compliance
Lightning Source LLC
Chambersburg PA
CBHW021148090426
42740CB00008B/1005